BEAUT
BRUGES

A Traveler's History

MADGE ATTWOOD

An Adrian Book
Davis, California

Beautiful Bruges: A Traveler's History
An Adrian Book/ January 2002

Library of Congress Cataloging-in-Publication Data

Library of Congress Control Number: 2001118739

Attwood, Madge
beautiful bruges: a traveler's history/ madge attwood

ISBN 0-9712787-0-9

Includes bibliographical references and index.
1. Bruges – History 1st to 21st centuries.2. Travel .

For my dear son, Chris, who believes I can do anything

In Appreciation

Roger Hoeman, retired architect of Bruges, generously reviewed the manuscript for historical accuracy and Alderman Hilde DeCleer brought me up-to-date on issues facing contemporary Bruges. The press department of Toerisme Brugge provided an official guide for a half day of exploring sites rarely reached by tourists. Gabriel Bossaer, the extraordinary guide, took me to secret corners of Bruges I could have never found on my own and gave an exhaustive history of every site. Noël Geirnaert, Archivist of the City Archives of Bruges, answered my many questions; Heidi Deneweth of the City Archives patiently translated Van Biervliet's article on the English presence in Bruges while I sat at her elbow in the archives taking notes. Professor Roger Weverbergh of the University of Utrecht supplied information about the history of Saint Donatian. Myrna, Chip, Jim, Crystle and Ted, my writing group partners, ruthlessly tore apart parts of the manuscript so I could put them back together in better form. Carl, Bob, David, Toba and Heather reviewed the manuscript and made invaluable comments that sharpened the final draft. Special thanks go to Piet Beul, who arranged for Mr. Hoeman to review the book, to Anne de Meerleer, Director of Press Relations for Toerisme Bruges who directed me to important resources, and to Lieve Jaspaert, Director of Press Relations for Bruges 2002, who introduced me to plans for the Culural Capital year.

Contents

BEAUTIFUL BRUGES
A Traveler's History

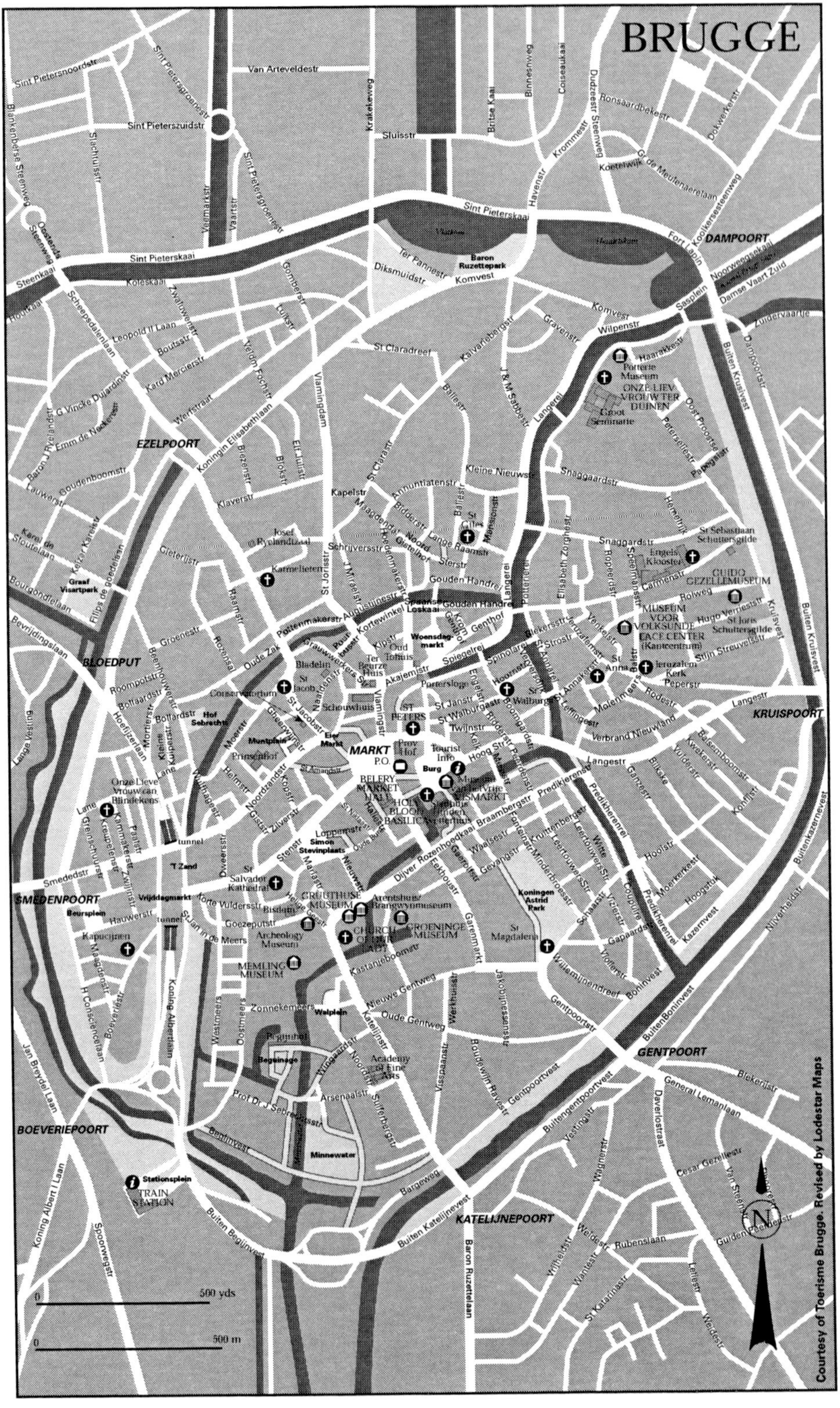

BRUGGE
DAMPOORT
EZELPOORT
BLOEDPUT
KRUISPOORT
SMEDENPOORT
GENTPOORT
BOEVERIEPOORT
KATELIJNEPOORT
MARKT
P.O.
Burg
Tourist Info
BELFRY
MARKET HALL
HOLY BLOOD BASILICA
Stadhuis
VISMARKT
ST PETERS
Woensdagmarkt
Spaanse Loskaai
Oud Tolhuis
Ter Beurze Huis
Bladelin
St Jacob
Schouwhuis
Prinsenhof
Eier Markt
Muntplein
Hof Sebrechts
Conservatorium
Karmelieten
Josef Rylandtzaal
St Gilles
Graaf Visartpark
Simon Stevinplaats
St Salvador Kathedraal
'T Zand
Vrijdagmarkt
Beursplein
Kapucijnen
Onze Lieve Vrouw van Blindekens
GRUUTHUSE MUSEUM
Arentshuis/ Brangwynmuseum
GROENINGE MUSEUM
CHURCH OF OUR LADY
Archeology Museum
MEMLING MUSEUM
Walplein
Begijnhof
Beguinage
Academy of Fine Arts
Minnewater
Stationsplein
TRAIN STATION
Koningin Astrid Park
St Magdalena
Jeruzalem Kerk
St Anna
St Walburga
MUSEUM VOOR VOLKSUNDE
LACE CENTER (Kantcentrum)
GUIDO GEZELLEMUSEUM
St Sebastiaan Schuttersgilde
St Joris Schuttersgilde
Engels Klooster
Potterie Museum
ONZE-LIEVE-VROUW TER DUINEN
Groot Seminarie
Baron Ruzettepark
Sint Pieterskaai
Komvest
Langestr
Smedestr
Koning Albertlaan
Buiten Katelijnevest
Buiten Begijnvest
Baron Ruzettelaan
Koningin Elisabethlaan
Vlamingstr
Hoogstr
Steenstr
Zuidzandstr
Noordzandstr
Dijver
Rozenhoedkaai
Katelijnestr
Mariastr
Gentpoortstr
Bargeweg
0
500 yds
0
500 m
N
Courtesy of Toerisme Brugge. Revised by Lodestar Maps

Preface

On my first visit to Bruges, I expected a well-done renaissance fair with costumed residents and a contrived replication of history. Instead I found an authentic historic city neither artificially engineered nor superficial. The restoration of its ancient buildings was architecturally honest and for the most part followed the intent of original builders.

In preparation for the trip I pored over Internet sites related to the city and consumed travel guides that raised more questions than they answered.

The more I read the more puzzled I became. I wondered who the Flemish were and from what people they evolved. Were they Gallic, Saxon, Celtic, or something else? I was curious about their seeming preoccupation with freedom and independence from earliest times, apparently in contrast to other nations of the period. France is their neighbor, yet why did I sense a rivalry with that country?

Who were the beguines? If not nuns and not under the heavy hand of the medieval Catholic Church, why did they even exist as a distinct community?

As I continued to read it seemed the city was repeatedly in a state of rebellion and conflict and I wondered why. How could it become the most prosperous center of finance and international trade for Northern Europe in the midst of such turmoil? What caused its deterioration? Some writers blamed it on the silting of the river Zwin. That alone seemed too simplistic an explanation.

I wondered how Bruges survived the excesses of the Reformation and the bombings of two world wars virtually unscathed when other European cities lost many of their ancient buildings and historical treasures. What led to its rebirth?

I hungered for details. Thinking others might share my curiosity, I have pulled together historical information which may fill some gaps for the traveler who finds travel guides too superficial and historical tomes too weighty. In the interest of readability I have not used footnotes. For those who wish to delve more deeply, the bibliography lists the sources I utilized. If you read French or Dutch, the archives of Bruges are a treasure trove of original material. A glossary on page 130 will clarify some terms that are not in common usage.

While many tourists try to experience Bruges on a day trip from Brussels or Antwerp, I do not believe you can fully appreciate the marvels of this remarkable city in so little time. Trailing after a guide in the company of twenty other tourists, breezing past the works of medieval masters and having lunch at a crowded café on the Markt may be charming diversions, but they are like glancing at chapter headings rather than reading a book.

The entire Center City is a work of art. In three days you may feel dizzy trying to absorb the town's riches. In a week you can wander the less traveled streets, spend quiet moments in the beguinage, pore over the masterpieces in the museums, and savor a variety of exquisite Belgian cuisine.

The April-May or September-October shoulder seasons are the best times to visit. In the warm months of June, July, and August a crush of tourists on day trips from other cities congests the streets, the sidewalks and the canal boats. On my second visit in February of 2001, the days were chilly but pleasant and the streets were not crowded.

If you can travel in May, time your visit to coincide with the Procession of the Holy Blood. More than a religious parade, it is colorful outdoor theater on a splendid scale.

On the other hand, if summer is your only option, try to begin an exploration of museums and historic buildings before 10:00 a.m. when the tour buses arrive and after 4:00 p.m. when they leave. The time between is grand for wandering among less popular sites.

I like to sit at an outdoor café sipping beer, eating mussels and Belgian fries and imagining what the town might have been like five or six hundred years ago. I like to feel the spirit of the city, to savor its special ambience. The Town Hall on the Burg appears much as it did in the 14th century and the ancient belfry on the Markt, the main square in the Center City, could be announcing the Joyous Entry of a new Burgundian ruler.

If you are a morning person, take an early walk in the predawn silence of the city and let your imagination run wild. Imagine you are a burgher meeting other merchants in front of the Van der Beurse house to set daily exchange rates or a knight of the Golden Fleece preparing for a visit from the King of France. Perhaps you are one of the townspeople who rioted after the murder of Count Charles the Good in 1127 A.D. or the wealthy, powerful politician and businessman Louis van Gruuthuse, leaving his mansion for a morning constitutional along the Dijver before receiving the English king, Edward IV. You might be the wife of a wealthy baker taking bread to poverty-stricken residents of the Baker's Guild almshouse on Minderbroedersstraat. Maybe a painter, a sculptor, or an illuminator of manuscripts sitting under a tree in the cool morning light or on the banks of the Minnewater planning your next masterpiece.

Since the best way to see Bruges is on foot, your first stop after getting settled should be the Tourist Office on the Burg. There you will find maps, brochures and guide services. You can sign up for a group tour of the most famous sites for a small fee or the bureau can arrange a private guide for an hourly rate.

Before beginning, however, a few cautions are in order. To make the most of your time I suggest that, in addition to gathering information about the city, you give attention to your feet. A memorable visit may be aided by securing a guide and visiting historical treasures, but comfort is critical. To paraphrase an old adage, the mind can only absorb what the feet can endure.

Ignore fashion. Wear thick soled, well-cushioned flat-heeled shoes and carry lots of moleskin with a small pair of scissors for cutting the protective material to shape.

Of course, if you are a masochist, thin-soled leather shoes with heels at least two inches high are required. Within an hour of walking on cobblestone streets your perfectly normal, happy feet will be transformed into howling appendages. After an hour of traversing cobblestones, two-inch heels will leave you feeling little better than being stretched on the rack and make you a great candidate for the sprained ankle set.

So put on your thick-soled, shock absorbing walking shoes and let us take a stroll through the history of beautiful Bruges.

Introduction

Eight miles inland from the North Sea, Bruges evokes visions of medieval life so striking it has been called a perfectly preserved medieval wonder; a jewel of the Middle Ages.

The graceful beauty of mirror-surfaced canals that weave through the Center City have led enraptured visitors to describe it as the Venice of the North. Picturesque stone bridges arch over the canals, the earliest built in 1294. Once serving foreign merchants who were transporting goods to be traded for Bruges' fine woolen textiles, waterways now carry visitors listening to amplified talks.

Cobblestone streets curve, run off at angles, and interlace in intricate patterns. The ancient belfry, the spire of Our Lady's Church, and the tower of Saint Savior's Cathedral create an awesome skyline.

Many of its people carry out their everyday activities in beautifully restored old buildings. They live in Gothic style houses from the 1500's and 1600's built of russet or ochre brick with quaint stepped-gable facades. Officials go about the business of governing the town from restored medieval buildings on the Burg, some dating from the 12th and 13th centuries. Restaurants and shops do business in structures constructed by craft and merchant guilds 500 years ago.

Nearly every street harbors secrets of the city's past. Over and over prosperity and growth alternated with rebellion and war. Misery and disease followed conflict and then prosperity and brilliance returned as the resilient Flemings picked themselves up and began all over again. Only at the end of the 1500's did irreversible decline set in. By mid-1800, the city, once the wealthiest financial center of Northern Europe, had become a poor provincial Flemish town.

On my first visit, I stopped for a cup of tea at the Laurent, a small café on the corner of Steenstraat and Saint Niklasstraat. The tearoom occupies a building whose gabled facade dates from the 17th century with a foundation that was probably laid in the 12th or 13th century.

The blue and yellow tearoom glowed with cheer and warmth. I ordered a Belgian waffle, then gazed onto the street, dazzled by history on every side. Across from the café, 9th century Saint Savior's Cathedral rose like a gray, hovering presence. I could almost see burghers in somber clothing and gloomy faces enter its huge doors.

Without warning, the street in front of the café exploded with shouts accompanied by the distant, rhythmic beating of drums. Curious, I hurried to the door. Bizarre faces painted blue and red and red and yellow with scarves and hats and shirts matching the faces filled the street from curb to curb.

Across from the tearoom a staggering youth, his face covered with blue and red stripes, faced another wearing a red and yellow flag around his shoulders like a cape. The one in blue and red gave red and yellow a shove. They exchanged words in two languages and seemed to be seconds from exchanging blows when the companion of the first stepped between them, spoke urgently to his friend and pulled him into a doorway. Moments later, subdued, the young man rejoined the crowd, glancing back at his opponent from time to time.

I asked the waiter what was happening. He laughed. "Today is the soccer playoff between Yugoslavia and Spain. The fans are in high spirits." I exhaled and let a smile drift across my face. Red and blue were Yugoslavia's colors, he explained, and red and yellow were Spain's. The rival teams would compete for the Euro 2000 soccer title that afternoon.

The river of bodies flowed on and energy filled the air like electricity. Later, surrounded by ancient buildings that carried the scent of history, modern youths swilled beer and bonded with each other in enthusiastic support for teams that would shortly compete for the Euro 2000 title. The games created such a wave of festivity and merrymaking I could envision the revelry in the Middle Ages when jousts and tournaments were in full sway.

Next morning the narrow streets were empty. A hushed calm pervaded the park where ancient Saint Donatian's Church once stood. The Town Hall dominated the Burg in mute Gothic splendor while 14th century Pieter de Coninc and Jan Breidel presided in silent bronze celebrity over the deserted Markt. An early morning mist hovered on the green surface of the Minnewater as snow-white swans soundlessly glided in formation over its placid surface. By 10:00 a.m. buses and trains from Brussels, Ghent and Antwerp belched tourists from their doors and the early morning serenity disappeared.

* * * * *

In the following pages, an imaginary Bruges historian, whom I shall call Anders Van der Meers, will recount the drama of Bruges' ascent into world renown, its descent into insignificance and its remarkable rebirth. He will present the story of Bruges within the broader context of Flanders and, at times, of the Southern Netherlands. Mr. Van der Meers and his granddaughter are fictitious; however, all other characters are real and actually lived in the periods described in the story.

Chapter One

"Let me introduce myself. My name is Anders Van der Meers." A slow smile curved his lips. "This old body refused to cooperate years ago but my mind is as sharp today as it was at age forty." A hint of pride danced in his eyes.

He paused for several seconds. "I know my remaining days are limited. That's why I've agreed to share some of what I know about my beloved Bruges.

"My granddaughter insists I live with her in Lille so I no longer have a home in Bruges, but my heart will always be there. A remarkable town. If its streets could talk, what tales they would tell."

The warm fragrance of baking cakes wafted through the house.

"Please join my granddaughter and me in the library. We'll sit over there near the fire to take the chill off. I love these crisp Belgian days. Settle into that old, soft chair and be comfortable for this will take a while. I'll take this one. It's so used to me, it follows all my sharp angles." He chuckled. "Here's Miriam now with wine and cakes for us."

I turned on my tape recorder after the wine was poured and asked if I might ask questions.

"Anything you like," he said, "but I won't guarantee a quick answer. Let's see. Where shall I begin?"

"Perhaps in the earliest times," I suggested.

"I guess we can do it chronologically. Of course you understand, I'll only touch on the highlights."

I nodded. "What if you start with the origin of the people?"

"Yes," he said. He became still and his eyes seemed to focus on something far in the past. Then he began, slowly, pensively.

* * * * *

"In pre-Christian times the people were Celtic and lived in a sparsely populated, scattered settlement. The area was mainly swampland and subject to recurring floods from the North Sea. Forests, marshes, and clay-like soil separated the region from eastern Flanders. As the Romans swept through Europe, they eventually reached the settlement that would become Bruges and built fortifications to protect the coast against pirate attacks. The Romans considered the settlement a remote frontier outpost and occupied the region from the 1st to the 5th centuries.

"In the settlement, two rivers flowed around an oblong island to a natural harbor where ships seeking haven from the violent storms of the North Sea frequently moored. Until the 11th century, ships were probably able to sail directly into the center of the town making trade and commerce a natural development.

"Sheep were easily raised on the dune heaths which suggests that a tradition of cloth making may have existed even from prehistoric times. Commerce with England and Gaul could have occurred as early as 100 A.D.

"When the Roman Empire collapsed in 476 A.D., the territory fell into the hands of the Franks, Germanic tribes from the north and east of The Netherlands. The Franks took possession of an area that roughly embraced present-day

Germany, Austria, Holland, Belgium, Luxembourg, France and part of Italy, ruling until 987 A.D.

"The great Charlemagne, King of the Franks and Emperor of the Holy Roman Empire, conquered lands that stretched from the Baltic Sea to the Mediterranean. When he died in 814 A.D., he bequeathed the empire to his son, Louis the Pious. After Louis died, his kingdom was eventually divided among his squabbling sons into the German Empire and the Western Kingdom of the Franks. In 850, Charles the Bald, son of Louis' second wife, received the Western Kingdom, an area that encompassed the Low Countries (Belgium, Holland and Luxembourg) and France.

"The breakup of Charlemagne's empire created rumblings of discontent among the people at the same time that Vikings were wreaking havoc on the coastlines. Charles the Bald was having difficulty maintaining the peace. Strong men on all sides took the uneasiness of the times as an opportunity to seize as much power as they could.

"Complicating matters for King Charles, the common people were putting less trust in royal bloodlines. In fact, anyone who possessed charisma and personal power, but who had not pledged loyalty to the king, was perceived as a threat to the monarchy.

"An adventurer of growing fame named Rotbert, rumored to be an obscure descendant of Charlemagne, was developing a core of supporters. Gosfried and Guntfried, two northern chiefs who were loyal to King Charles and who exerted considerable influence over him, urged the king to bind Rotbert to him rather than risk his developing an opposition following. The king agreed, received Rotbert in court, accepted his homage, and made him a vassal, not realizing he was laying the foundation of a rival house.

"Rotbert had great tact and diplomacy and his influence continued to grow. Despite the pledge of loyalty he had made to the king, the chiefs saw his increasing power as dangerous and were determined to bring him down.

"With the support of Louis, King Charles' son, and Judith, his accomplished daughter, they sent an urgent summons to Baldwin Iron Arm, a northern chief renowned for his cleverness and prowess in battle. (Apparently people called him Iron Arm because he rarely removed his coat of mail). The king, they said, needed help in dealing with a possible usurper of the throne. Without hesitation, Baldwin mounted his horse and sped to France.

"Judith, King Charles' daughter, an intelligent and beautiful woman, had been widowed twice although she was only twenty years old. Both husbands had been Saxon kings and Alfred, son of her first husband, the King of Wessex, became the revered Alfred the Great. She was a remarkable woman and, according to some, as stepmother responsible for Alfred's early training, helped mold him into the superb ruler he later became.

"Judith returned to France from England after the death of her second husband. In Senlis, she lived in luxury appropriate to her station under the protection of the bishops of Senlis. Despite the opulence of her surroundings, however, she was virtually a prisoner, a pawn for the extension of her father's empire. Rulers in those days used their daughters to seal alliances with other nations by marrying them off to the sons of foreign kings. The children of the union would ultimately become heirs to the king's lands.

"Baldwin Iron Arm and Judith met when Baldwin arrived in France and the couple fell in love soon after. They wanted to wed, but unfortunately, love was an insufficient reason for marrying, especially since Baldwin was only a tribal chief. Knowing approval of her father was impossible, the couple eloped and fled to the court of her cousin Lothar in the Rhineland.

"Furious, King Charles arranged their excommunication and demanded the couple's extradition under an agreement he had made with Lothar for the exchange of criminals.

"Baldwin retaliated by threatening to join the Viking pirates who were attacking and plundering the northern coast of Charles' kingdom.

"The Scandinavian pirates, mostly Danes, pillaged churches, looted monasteries and seized agricultural land from peaceful farmers. Their long boats had shallow drafts that enabled them to sail far up the rivers of Western Europe. Holding thirty to forty warriors, each vessel was capable of a formidable attack.

"For Baldwin to join the Norsemen would be a terrible blow to the king, already fearful the heathen bands would overrun his kingdom.

"Perhaps Judith softened her lover's anger or perhaps he decided on his own not to act in haste, because the couple journeyed to Rome to present their case before the Pope. They earnestly wanted the blessing of the Church and of Judith's father, King Charles the Bald.

"For the Pope, the marriage of Baldwin and Judith was of little consequence. Judith had eloped; she had not been kidnapped. However, the possibility of Baldwin joining the Vikings was a grave danger. Pope Nicholas recognized their marriage and urged Baldwin to return to the North and assist in the king's defense against the Vikings.

"With great reluctance, Charles the Bald finally agreed to allow the excommunication to be lifted and the marriage to be solemnized. Baldwin and Judith were formally married in a sumptuous ceremony in Auxerre, France, with the ministers and officers of state for King Charles present. The only disappointment was her stubborn father's refusal to attend.

However, at the Pope's insistence, the king conferred the highest honors on Baldwin.

"The couple journeyed north to the outlying domains of the king, committed to protecting the territory from Viking invasion."

Anders reached for his wine glass. After a long sip, he continued.

"When Baldwin and Judith arrived in the land over which the king had given them authority, they chose the tiny coastal settlement known as Bruggia, a collection of cottages around a crumbling fortress. The surrounding countryside, covered with heath and scrub, supported large flocks of sheep owned by various abbeys. Some authorities think Baldwin had lived in Bruggia during the ten years before he eloped with Judith, but records are unclear.

"Bruggia, the embryonic Bruges of later centuries, was a lonely, desolate place, hemmed in by forest and marshland. The settlement itself was situated on an island enclosed on two sides by a river. Nevertheless, it was, to Baldwin's thinking, a good place to establish a stronghold to fend off the Danes.

"Bruggia became the birthplace of Flanders, the northern territory King Charles gave Baldwin authority to rule. Baldwin Iron Arm became the first count of Flanders.

"He built a spacious, fortified castle on the island and surrounded the castle complex with a strong, high wall that could only be entered through four gates. Each gate was protected by a portcullis; a heavy, iron, lattice-like structure that could be raised or lowered as need arose. The castle complex held the count's residence, that of his officials, a place to lodge hostages, a chapel, and a prison.

"Around the periphery of the settlement clustered the houses, huts and hovels of the people who served the castle and the church.

"From the castle, Baldwin was prepared to defend the king's northern territory. However, instead of fighting the Vikings, he found he was able to buy them off and enjoyed a lull in their ongoing assaults.

"Opposite the castle and its auxiliary buildings, he founded a sanctuary dedicated to Our Lady to receive the relics of Saint Donatian, patron saint of Bruges. The Archbishop of Rheims had given the relics to Baldwin some time before and Baldwin had sent them for safekeeping to the clerics of Torhout. The clerics, seeking protection from the Vikings, delivered the precious relics when the sanctuary was built. In the 900's, Baldwin's grandson, Arnulf I, built the famous Saint Donatian's Church on the site of the sanctuary."

The old gentleman leaned back, placed his elbow on the arm of the chair, and rested his chin on his hand.

After a moment he said, "Baldwin's descendants ruled Flanders for almost 300 years."

Oldest Bruges

River Dijver between Gruuthuse Museum and Johannes Nepomucenus Bridge

How to get there from the Burg: As you leave the Visitors Bureau, turn left, then left again onto Blinde Ezelstraat. Follow Blinde Ezelstraat past the Fish Market to its end, about two blocks. This is Braambergstraat. Turn right on Braambergstraat. In two blocks, the name changes to Dijver. You are now standing in the oldest section of the city. Across the street are the Gruuthuse, Brandwyn, Arents, and Groeninge Museums. Note these for later visits. At

Wollestraat, to your right as you face the canal, picturesque Saint John Nepomucenus Bridge crosses the Dijver Canal.

Possible location of the first Gallo-Roman fortress and Baldwin I's castle complex

From Saint John Nepomucenus Bridge, turn right on Rozenhoedkaai if you are facing the canal, and follow it to Huidenvettersplein. Turn left; walk through the square, and at the canal you will be on Steenhouwersdijk. The street will become Groenerei. Note the Pelikaan almshouses on the right as you follow Groenerei. The street will curve to the right.

Continue on to the bridge that crosses the canal at Predikherenstraat. Cross the bridge and immediately turn left. At Langestraat, turn left again, cross another bridge and turn right onto Verversdijk. You will now be beside the Sint Annarei Canal. When Sint Annarei makes a sharp turn, follow the canal to the left. You should be on Spinolarei. The Kraanrei, the canal that formed the fourth side of the square island was filled in a number of years ago.

Spinolarei will take you past the Biskajersplein and onto Kraanplein. Kraanplein will end at Vlamingstraat. Turn left and continue along Vlamingstraat to the Markt. Vlamingstraat ends at the Markt. Cross the square and enter Wollestraat. Wollestraat takes you back to Saint John Nepomucenus Bridge. The square area you have just circumscribed on foot is hypothesized to have been the location of an original Gallo-Roman fortress that was in ruins by the time Baldwin established his castle complex. Baldwin's castle is believed to have been built on what is now the Burg.

To reach the Burg from here, face away from the canal and turn left. Turn left again onto Blinde Ezelstraat, cross the canal and continue straight ahead to the Burg.

Across the square is a small park. Here you will find a scale model of Saint Donatian's on the original site of the church. French revolutionaries destroyed the cathedral during the 18th and 19th century occupation of Bruges. Go into the lobby of the Holiday Inn Crown Plaza and downstairs to view the remains of old Saint Donatian's. The ruins were discovered during excavations for construction of the hotel.

Chapter Two

"That's an amazing story," I said. "But what happened to Rotbert?"

"Ah yes. Rotbert became Count of Anjou and then Abbot of Tours, consolidating his power. He ultimately founded the royal house of France."

"What a turn! Then he eventually destroyed King Charles' dynasty?"

"That's right."

We sat quietly for several moments as I digested the twists and turns of history.

"What was Bruges like in those days? I asked. "Was the count like a dictator with supreme authority?"

"No, not at all. Most European regions submitted to feudalism for protection against robber bands that were terrorizing the continent. Although under the umbrella of feudalism, the people of Flanders had their own laws, almost independent of the authorities who nominally ruled over them.

"In 993, Count Baldwin III sowed the seeds for an organized democratic tradition that continued for centuries. He divided Flanders into small administrative districts, each headed by a castellan who governed the settlements around the castles or forts and represented him. The stronghold from which the castellan exerted authority was independent. The count did not directly control it.

"The castellan and members of the castellan's council made day to day decisions. In later centuries, a mayor and aldermen would govern the city and the castellan would govern the rural areas. There was no central administration for the region although the count granted rights and privileges to each city and governing unit as he saw fit. Every city had a militia whose role was to protect the district. The count had the right to call the citizen army into service at any time to supplement his larger armies. He also had the right to collect taxes to support his wars and other pursuits. Negotiation of rights and privileges as a condition of support for the count was common practice.

"So the local leaders retained a measure of control over their rulers," I said.

"Yes, to a certain extent."

For several moments, Anders stared out a window that framed a peaceful green meadow as if reflecting on some unseen vista.

"Flanders was a violent place. To show loyalty to one's family, members promptly avenged threats. Feuds to settle differences were commonplace.

"The count gave church courts responsibility for judging damage done by feuds or private wars instead of having those problems handled by civil courts. If a clan member was found guilty of murdering someone during a private war, mild discipline was typically meted out. However, if the murdered victim was one with whom a sacred relationship existed, e.g., father, mother, priest or abbot, the penalties were grave.

"Occasionally the count, rather than the church court, assigned gruesome penalties in order to make an example. In one incident, the count ordered a knight burned alive who had stolen two cows from a farm woman.

"A later count had a knight boiled in oil and ten others hanged as punishment for violating the peace of a fair at Torhout.

"Retaining and strengthening their power bases were major preoccupations of the counts. They did this by giving land to nobles who supported their policies. To have sufficient land to give away, they had to enlarge their holdings by propitious marriages to royal women who could bring a rich dowry of land to the union or by forcibly taking land that belonged to other countries. Sometimes the reverse occurred of course, and they found themselves having to call on the militias to help protect their own borders from invaders.

"Baldwin IV succeeded his father in 988 and granted liberties to Bruges that caused trade to expand at a phenomenal rate. Merchants from foreign ports found the business climate so attractive, the town became an important center of commerce.

"Less than 100 years later, however, a great catastrophe occurred that seriously jeopardized the city's trading position. From the 7th or 8th centuries, dikes had been built along the coastline to prevent flooding of the lowlands during the fierce winter storms of the North Sea. The fertile land left behind was drained and reclaimed from the sea for farming. In the second half of the 11th century, land reclamation caused Bruges' access to the sea to silt up and its harbor, crucial for trade, was lost.

"The resourceful burghers were not easily dissuaded from their profitable commercial relationships, however. They conducted business by overland routes instead of the sea and their industries survived."

Chapter Three

"Did Bruges continue to grow?" I asked.

"Yes, it did," he said. "Trade kept expanding and Bruges was becoming an important center of commerce. Fortunes had been made and a core of wealthy families now dominated the town. The ragged settlement that Baldwin I took over had become a bustling community.

"In 1119 A.D., Count Baldwin VII was dying and he had no children to inherit his lands. On his deathbed, he named his cousin, Charles of Denmark, to succeed him. Charles was a mature man who had been in the Flemish court since 1086. His father had been a Danish king and his mother was Flemish.

"After Charles became count, he developed a reputation as a ruler with great compassion for the less fortunate whom he treated with extraordinary courtesy and kindness. He gave sympathy and protection to the indigent, founded hospitals and asylums to ease their suffering, built monasteries and churches for their spiritual well being, and presided over regal feasts for the blind and crippled. Not surprisingly, he became well loved."

"But I understand Charles the Good was murdered," I said. "How could it happen when he was so popular?"

"He was popular among the poor, but a threat to some who were in positions of power. He was an astute politician and an advocate of law and order, but his position was in opposition to Bruges' long-standing tradition of violence and private wars for settling disputes.

"An immensely wealthy and violent clan, the Erembalds, had dominated the city's administration for many years from headquarters on the Burg. The Provost of Saint Donatian's Church, an arrogant, powerful Erembald, held the post of Chancellor of Flanders, and even substituted for the count in the ruler's absence.

"The Erembalds' wealth and power rivaled that of Count Charles. Their wealth was so great they could have bought places in the nobility, but privately they scorned the notion. They were contemptuous of the entire feudal system and with good reason. From a fiercely proud family with a history of lawlessness, the clan had, over the decades, accumulated their wealth through plunder and commerce. They were descended from the wild, barbarous Karls who once inhabited a strip of land along the coast of Flanders and, like their forebears, held freedom and independence dearer than life.

"Charles, on the other hand, valued law and order more than personal freedom. Naturally, the Erembalds opposed his reforms at every turn. When he issued an edict that only his officers could be armed in time of peace, an order intended to promote law and order and a seemingly minor issue, the clan was outraged. They considered bearing arms the right of every free man and to rescind that right was tantamount to fostering rebellion.

"For many years, the Erembalds had been involved in a feud with the Stratens, another powerful and wealthy family. The head of the Straten clan was both a member of the count's Privy Council and the count's friend and confidante.

"A deputation of peasants who were retainers of the Stratens complained to the count that the Erembalds, led by Burchard, nephew of the Provost of Saint Donatian, had ravaged their homes, devastated their land and driven off their cattle. Charles promised them justice. After consultation with his advisors, he ordered Burchard's house burned to the ground.

"Some time earlier he had issued a proclamation that 'a freeman who married a serf should, after a year's wedlock sink to his wife's condition.' Why he issued the order is not known, but because of the order, any Erembald who had ever married a serf was legally a serf, irrespective of his current position. Since intermarriage was common over the years, the edict reduced most of the clan to that rank.

"In the feudal hierarchy, serfs were the lowest social class, relegated to service to their liege lord. Thus, legally, the Erembalds were servants of Count Charles. A serf was not free and enjoyed none of the privileges of freemen.

"The Erembalds ignored the law although their altered status was an open secret among ruling officials of other territories who did not consider it a troublesome issue. Charles, however, was apparently unaware that they were no longer freemen until advised by the court. He was elated. They belonged to him; they were his servants to do with as he chose no matter how great their wealth or prestige.

"The Erembalds were horrified. The court's judgment endangered their freedom and threatened their positions of influence in the city, positions they had held for over 100 years. They saw the action as an attempt to ruin them and sent a deputation to the count urging him to lift the onerous edict. Charles stood firm, claiming he could not go against the court's decision.

"The clan were convinced all avenues for reconciliation had been exhausted. They believed the count's refusal to relent left only one alternative. In secret, they began to plan the ruler's death.

"In the early hours of March 2, 1127, Charles went to Saint Donatian's Church, as was his practice, and knelt in prayer before the Lady's Altar. Burchard, whose house the count had ordered destroyed, sneaked up behind the ruler, sword in hand, delivered a single blow, and Charles instantly fell dead."

"What hatred!" I exclaimed. "How did the people respond?"

"The whole city erupted in an uproar. Fear and confusion gripped the entire populace.

"The Erembalds were afraid that riots and vengeance would follow if the funeral were held in the town so they let the count's body lay unburied in Saint Donatian's for three days while they tried to decide what to do with it.

"Finally, they asked Arnulph, Abbot of Blandinium in Ghent to secretly deliver Charles' body to his cloister and there give it a Christian burial.

"Somehow word got out. You must remember that at this time superstition was widespread, especially about the powers of holy relics. The audacity of taking their benefactor's body to another city horrified the grieving citizens.

"Arnulph and the Erembalds carried the body down the aisle of the cathedral, confident their scheme would work, but before they reached the door, the tramping of feet and the sound of angry voices made their blood run cold. The doors of the church burst open to a terrifying scene. All of Bruges had turned out to prevent the removal of their beloved count.

"The following morning Arnulph chanted a solemn Requiem Mass in Saint Peter's Church and Count Charles the Good was laid to rest where he was murdered, in front of the Lady Altar in the Cathedral of Saint Donatian.

"How the Erembalds thought they could succeed in carrying out such a deed without retribution is a mystery. Perhaps in their arrogance they believed they had power greater than the people's when, in reality, their power base was far smaller. They could not possibly defend themselves against an entire town filled with citizens in a murderous rage.

"The crowd cried for vengeance, vowing to hunt down and kill every Erembald. In the weeks of ruthless reprisal that followed, the Erembalds attempted to flee the city. Of those who succeeded, every single one was eventually found by the maniacal mob and killed. The provost, once the most respected official in the city, was hunted like an animal and brutally murdered.

"Frightened by the continuing violence, the citizens of Bruges fortified the stone wall around the city to give it a stronger measure of protection. The wall stood for two centuries."

We were both silent for a time as I absorbed his words. I wondered if vengeance was ever worth the cost.

A smile creased my face as I glanced at the old scholar. His head had drooped and a soft snore broke the silence.

Location of the Wall Strengthened After the Murder of Charles the Good

From the Burg: Take Blinde Ezelstraat to Rozenhoedkaai. The canal you crossed is the Dijver. The city wall followed the canals that encircled the city. We will trace the approximate location of the old wall by following the canals as far as possible. Since some canals have been filled in, we will go only as far as Zuidzandstraat.

If you are facing the buildings, not the canal, turn left and follow the canal to Huidenvettersplein. Turn left at the restaurants and proceed to the canal. The street name beside the canal is Steenhouwersdijk and will change to Groenerei. Continue on to the bridge that crosses the canal at Predikherenstraat. Cross the bridge and make a sharp left on Predikherenstraat. On Langestraat, cross another bridge and turn right on Verversdijk. You are now beside the Sint Annarei Canal. Follow the canal to Carmersstraat. Cross the bridge and jog right to Gouden-Handrei. The street name will change to Spanse Loksai. The canals you are following formed a moat around the 12th century defensive walls.

At Spanjaardstraat, turn right, cross the bridge and turn left on Augustijnenrei. The great painters van Eyck, Memling, and Pourbus lived in this area although their houses no longer exist. Note that the area is close to the wealthy district where foreign merchants had their headquarters. The street becomes Pottenmakersstraat after it intersects with Vlamingstraat. On Pottenmakersstraat, look across the canal toward Pieterpourbusstraat. You will see a tower from the 12th century wall in the garden wall of a house on Pieterpourbusstraat.

Cross to the other side of the canal at Ezelstraat and turn right on Moerstraat. Follow the canal as closely as possible all the way to Zuidzandstraat. You are now at the Zand, a square used for meetings, executions, jousts, and tournaments in the early years of Bruges. The Zand was outside the city walls at the time the first defensive city wall was constructed.

Saint Peter's Chapel

Saint Peter's Church, in which the Requiem Mass for Charles the Good was celebrated, is believed to have been built by Robert the Frisian in the 11th century, demolished in the 18th century and later rebuilt.

It can be reached as follows: take Burgstraat on the Burg to

Philipstockstraat. Turn left and follow Philipstockstraat to Keersstraat. Turn right.

Chapter Four

"I keep hearing that silting of the River Zwin caused the decline of Bruges. Can you enlighten me about that?"

"First of all," he said, "you need to know that the silting of the Zwin was only one of many events that led to the city's decline and possibly not even the most important. To understand the river's significance we need to continue in the 12th century.

"In 1134, seven years after the death of Count Charles, an enormous flood along the coast scooped out a long channel deep enough for navigation by large ships from the North Sea to Damme creating the River Zwin. You may remember that land reclamation over the centuries had made Bruges an inland city. Since Bruges and Damme are only three kilometers apart, a canal was excavated between the towns facilitating the free flow of foreign goods into Bruges from sea-going vessels. Although commodities had to be transferred to smaller crafts that could maneuver the canal, international trade expanded dramatically. However, the Zwin's tendency to silt up required periodic dredging to maintain navigability, a practice that would continue until the 1400's.

"Over the years, fine woolen textiles woven from high quality English wool earned Bruges a reputation for producing premium quality woolen cloth that continued for centuries. Sheep had been raised in Flanders for hundreds of years, but they produced wool too coarse to make fine cloth. English wool from sheep bred for long silky fibers had the quality

Brugean weavers required. Demand for Bruges' textiles and the city's relatively easy maritime access brought foreign traders who fueled employment and prosperity. Merchants and entrepreneurs who bought the wool, hired weavers to make the cloth, then sold the finished product to the foreigners, accumulated substantial wealth."

"With prosperity from the textile industry, the city must have blossomed," I said.

"That's right," he said. "The city grew at an astounding rate. The appearance and expansion of churches was testimony to the town's affluence and burgeoning population. It now had four parish churches: Saint Savior's, Church of Our Lady, Saint Donatian's, and Saint Basil's.

"Our Lady's may have been originally built in the 9th century, but records are sketchy. At any rate, we know it was remodeled in the 1100's and rebuilt as a gothic church starting in the 1200's.

"Saint Savior's, the oldest, dates from the 9th century. It was totally reconstructed between the late 13th century and the first half of the 16th century. Little of the original structure remains today.

"Saint Donatian's was completely rebuilt after a fire in 1184 and demolished after French revolutionaries took over Flanders in 1795.

"Count Thierry, who succeeded Charles the Good, started building Saint Basil's in 1134. The Romanesque church was completed in 1157, but by the 19th century, the upper level was badly decayed. It was rebuilt in the popular neo-gothic style of that period. The lower level has been preserved in its original form.

"During the first half of the 13th century, a crystal vial of dark ruby fluid, said to be the water in which Joseph of Arimathea washed blood from the body of Christ, was brought to Bruges and placed in Saint Basil's Church.

"Some insist Count Thierry brought the relic from Jerusalem after his participation in the second crusade. Others argue it came from Constantinople and was brought by Count Baldwin IX who plundered that city and served as its Emperor in 1204 and 1205. Whatever the truth, the venerated relic was enshrined in the church now called the Chapel of the Holy Blood.

"Another sign of the city's affluence, Saint John's Hospital, was finished in the 1100's filling a desperate need for treating the sick and injured. Hospitals in those days were not only for the sick. They also provided shelter to passers-by, vagrants, pilgrims, the homeless, and the mentally ill. Although monks and nuns cared for the people who sought refuge, the city administered the institution.

"The city's appearance was quite different from that of today. Wooden houses with thatched roofs lined the unpaved streets. Devastating fires were so common, flammable roofs in certain districts were prohibited in 1232. After several fires in 1417 laid waste to parts of the city, subsidies were given to homeowners who replaced thatched roofs with tile. In the 16th century the building of wooden houses was prohibited altogether. Two wooden houses from the 15th century remain, however. You can still see them at #90 Vlamingstraat and #7 Genthof."

Chapel of the Holy Blood and Saint Basil's Church

The Basilica of the Holy Blood and Saint Basil's Church on the Burg are a double chapel. The 19th century neo-gothic Basilica is on the second level. Romanesque Saint Basil's is on the ground floor. The reliquary for the famous Holy Blood relic may be viewed in the museum of the Basilica.

Saint Savior's Cathedral

To reach Saint Savior's from the Burg, take Breidelstraat to the Markt, and then follow Steenstraat to Saint Savior's, the large gray cathedral on the left. The interior walls are covered with 17th century paintings, many by Van Oost. Works by Dirk Bouts and Hugo Van der Goes may be seen in the cathedral museum. As you walk around the church, note the magnificent tapestries on the walls, the marble tombs of church officials, and the escutcheons of the Knights of the Golden Fleece hung above the choir stalls,

Church of Our Lady

This church is at the corner of Dijver and Mariastraat. From Saint Savior's, retrace your steps to the Markt, then to the Burg and once more follow Blinde Ezelstraat to Rosenhoedkaai, the street that parallels the Dijver canal. Turn right on Rosenhoedkaai and follow it to The Church of Our Lady, approximately four blocks and on the left. The street name has changed to Dijver. Observe the magnificent church tower. We will return to the interior later.

Saint John's Hospital

From the Church of Our Lady, turn left on Mariastraat. The church is at the corner of Dijver and Mariastraat. Saint John's Hospital is across the street. Visit the 12th century hospital wards and the 17th century pharmacy located in the former monastery. Note the beautiful gothic dispensary. We will return later to the Memling Museum located in the chapel.

Chapter Five

"Can you tell me about the beguines? I asked. "And why so many priests and bishops were against them?"

Anders looked at me with his clear blue eyes, then laughed. "They didn't follow the rules," he said.

"In 1244, educated women in Bruges who were alone, who had independent means, and who were also devout Catholics established a small settlement near the Minnewater. It became a magnet for women who wanted to serve God as the apostles had done without all the politics and corruption of the 13th century Church. They were people of high morals, deep religious devotion, and genuine compassion who wanted simply to love themselves, to love God and to love others.

"There was one problem. They set their own rules without consulting church fathers and quietly avoided submitting to the Church's authority and control."

"That doesn't seem so outrageous. Why did they feel the need to organize? Couldn't they have joined an order of nuns and accomplished the same things?"

"I'll come to that in a minute," he said. "Be patient."

Admonished, I leaned back in my chair and waited.

"Margaret of Constantinople, Countess of Flanders, granted the beguinage full parish status in 1245. She subsidized the community and gave it the right to have its own parish church. I think it significant that the town council rather than the Church was given jurisdiction. The priests of Our Lady's, Holy Savior's and Saint Michael's were outraged and complained bitterly to the Pope, with little effect. Complaints to the Pope about beguines were commonplace."

"But why?" I asked.

"I'm getting to it."

"In the early Middle Ages, women of noble families had considerable personal power and public authority. They were abbesses and landholders, but by the 12th century, a concerted effort by church and civil authorities excluded them from public life. The few avenues of expression available were removed, leaving them confined to the home or the cloister.

"Men of the nobility and church fathers knew little about women as a whole, yet they defined their roles. If a woman was of the nobility, she was expected to marry or enter the convent. It was even permissible for her to become the mistress of a nobleman. If she was from an ordinary family, she had to become the perfect virgin, a competent, obedient wife, or a nun. Yet the convent was denied to many since it required a huge dowry for admittance.

If she did not fit any of these expectations, she was looked down on and suspected of having loose morals.

"Adding to their plight, husbands often abandoned their wives to join the crusades or other wars. Women widowed or left alone had no protection at a time when violence was common as eating. In the Middle Ages, a woman without a man was especially vulnerable to physical attack. Furthermore, a middle class woman was economically dependent on her husband and often unable to earn a living on her own.

"Nor was finding a husband a simple matter for an unmarried woman. The wars created a shortage of marriageable men."

"Do I detect a shade of anger in your voice?" I asked.

"Maybe," he said. "My great-granddaughter is studying medicine and sometimes I wonder what would have happened if she had lived then instead of now.

"But back to the story. The beguine movement met a need of women that neither the Church nor society was paying attention to. It provided protection, freedom of worship, a sense of belonging and, for some, a way to support themselves. The presence of the beguinage also added a much needed dimension of calm to a turbulent town. Today, it is one of the most peaceful spots in the city."

"Did you know that "beguine" was originally a derogatory name?" I shook my head. "It became permanent and evolved into a respectful title.

"Beguines took vows of chastity and obedience but not of poverty and the vows were not lifelong. They were permitted to change their minds at any time and leave the community. If a beguine was without an independent income, she would support herself by working in the textile industry, caring for the sick and orphans, or by making handicrafts. In the 16th century some became expert lacemakers and were active in choral service.

"Beguines were medieval feminists. They were forerunners of modern feminism. Thinking women who made their own decisions independently without obsequious deference to the church hierarchy. It took courage to step outside conventions of that day and endure the rage of the clergy.

"Powerlessness to dominate and control these clever, devout women shook the clerical community.

"As a gift to the beguines in 1299, King Philip the Fair of France removed the beguinage from municipal control and placed it under his direct authority. Since then it has been known as the "Princely Beguinage."

"When the last beguine died in the early 1900's, the convent was taken over by Benedictine nuns. Although they are committed to preserving some of the traditions of the beguines, the nuns, as you know, are under the authority of the Roman Catholic Church.

The Beguinage

Proceed from the Burg to Rosenhoedkaai; turn right. Follow the street to Mariastraat. Our Lady's Church will be on the left; Saint John's Hospital is around the corner. Continue on Mariastraat to Wijngaardstraat on the right. Turn right on Wijngaardstraat and follow it to the bridge that signals the entrance to the beguinage. The canal and bridge are on the right. Take a few moments to sit on one of the park benches facing the canal and watch the swans groom themselves on the grass and glide soundlessly by on the water.

The museum gift shop is on the right as you enter the gate to the beguinage. Stop here and get a booklet that explains the history of the complex. The interior of a medieval house in which a beguine lived is part of the museum. It is to the left of the gate as you enter. You can get a feeling for the simplicity of beguine life in the tiny rooms. Note that access to the beguinage is only over the bridge. In the Middle Ages, the canal created a moat and the walls provided added protection. The gate would be locked at night or in times of conflict.

You may see nuns scurrying to or from matins, vespers, or other services at the parish church during the day. In nice weather, a nun often sits outside her tiny house making lace. Take time to walk quietly around the elm dotted park. In spring, it is carpeted with brilliant yellow daffodils.

Leaving the beguinage, turn right after crossing the bridge. A few yards beyond is a lake-like expanse of water. This is the Minnewater or "Lake of Love" as romantics like to call it. Linguists recently translated Minnewater as "water where a sprite lives," however.

Sit on one of the benches beside the canal or the lake and reflect on all you have seen so far, then go to one of the restaurants on Wijngaardstraat and treat yourself to mussels, Belgian fries, and a cool glass of Straffe Hendrik beer. Beer is the national drink. One of Bruges' breweries makes 300 different varieties.

Chapter Six

"The 13th century must have been an exciting period with trade booming and the town growing," I said.

"You're partially right. Times were prosperous, but mounting tension clouded the era.

"Craft and merchant guilds thrived. Many guild members did extremely well and the guilds began to develop an important power base in the city. A weaver's guild, a butcher's guild, a painter's guild, a baker's guild and many more sprang up. They set quality standards, protected the privileges granted by the counts, and helped members who had fallen on hard times.

"The weaver's guild established rules for textile quality, inspected the textiles for excellence of workmanship and prohibited public competition among its members. This kind of quality control ensured that Bruges' reputation would remain intact. Goods that met its strict requirements received a stamp of approval placed directly on the fabric. Merchants purchased the fine quality cloth of master weavers and exported it to France, Spain, Italy, Portugal, and other distant lands.

"Aldermen of Bruges had to belong to the London Hanse, an umbrella organization of Flemish merchants in London that expedited trade with England. The problem with this requirement was that only merchants and entrepreneurs could be Hanse members. Guild masters, no matter how wealthy, were excluded and thus were denied aldermen's seats. Consequently, merchants dominated the city council, a source of great irritation to guild members who believed merchants had too much power.

"In 1270, Countess Margaret, the current ruler, added to the unrest by precipitating a rupture with England that produced an economic crisis. Margaret confiscated English property in Flanders, supposedly for non-payment of fees due her from the English, and the English queen retaliated by placing an embargo on trade with Flanders. Not until 1274 was the conflict resolved and trade resumed.

"Since the textile industry was dependent on English wool, business suffered. However, the situation did not become desperate. Traders smuggled English wool across the channel and their businesses stayed afloat, although it was not an ideal solution. Availability was unpredictable and quantities were limited.

"Despite this temporary setback, Bruges continued to thrive and flowered into the international trading and finance hub of northern Europe. Foreign traders were a continuing presence and often made Bruges their headquarters. Textiles dominated the foreign market, but art was also becoming an important enterprise. Manuscript illumination and the painting of miniatures for export were growing in popularity. Many citizens became wealthy.

"Guy de Dampierre succeeded Countess Margaret on her abdication in 1278. Since he was a patron of the arts and literature, he encouraged these pursuits and they grew increasingly important under his rule.

"In 1280, the silting of the Zwin became so serious that ocean-going vessels could no longer navigate the river into Damme, a serious problem for the city's continuing affluence. Count Guy, in cooperation with Bruges, solved the problem by founding Sluis as the new outport for Bruges. Large ships moored at Sluis, transferred their cargoes to smaller vessels that could navigate the Zwin as they had done at

Damme, and then made their way to Bruges. Trade continued to flourish.

"Nevertheless, tension in the city rose to a dangerous pitch between 1280 and 1302. A wealthy elite dominated the town and a prosperous but dissatisfied middle class emerged. Equally serious, an appalling gulf existed between the living standards of the rich and those of the poor. Poor people living in the city suffered grave hardships.

"For decades, onerous taxes and forced loans had supported the luxurious life styles of the counts and financed their wars of acquisition. The people resented the burdens placed on them by their rulers and social unrest was turning to agitation.

"Adding to the smoldering discontent, the wealthy upper class became jealous of the increasing affluence of the middle class. This was a very human reaction perhaps, but a surprising one nonetheless, since the upper class monopolized all the high municipal positions and every post of profit and advancement. Perhaps they feared losing their privileged status as the middle class became more powerful."

Anders paused and sipped his wine, thinking. After a moment, he continued.

"Count Guy added to the tension by siding with German traders in a dispute with the two families that held the weighing fief in Bruges, a privilege permitting the charge of tolls on imports according to weight. The Germans appealed to the Count, accusing the families of inconsistent administration of the privilege. The count sided with the Germans and in 1280 gave them generous weighing privileges in Aardenburg. The Germans left, stretching the tension of the burghers to the breaking point.

"Guy then left for a five-month visit to France, placing his son Robert in charge. During the count's absence, the aldermen stirred up dissatisfaction until it erupted in open rebellion. Mobs imprisoned men loyal to the count, burghers took over the city council, and from Robert, they demanded seats for guild masters on the board of aldermen and in the council.

"Victory was short-lived. The count returned, enraged at what had happened in his absence. He ruthlessly crushed the rebellion, imposed a huge cash indemnity on the city, and required compensation for damage done to his property and that of his loyal followers. As the final blow, he replaced the city charter with one that limited the town's autonomy. The original charter had been lost when the old wooden belfry in which it was kept burned to the ground during the uprising. The new charter abolished customs, gave the count authority to punish violent crimes as he chose and contained many punitive provisions. He then imprisoned the leaders of the rebellion and beheaded five."

"Good grief," I said. "That was a heavy handed move."

"And a foolish one," said Anders. "He would have been better served by listening to his peoples' complaints and entering into negotiations with the city fathers.

"By 1294, England and France were at war. Count Guy resisted demands for aid made by the French king, Philip, and refused a summons to appear before the French parliament. In 1296, he openly allied with England and renounced Flanders' feudal contract with France, enumerating his grievances and accusing the king of violating his duties to a loyal vassal.

"In early 1297, the governing oligarchies of Bruges, Ypres and Ghent took their own complaints against the count to the king. King Philip responded by withdrawing the new charter that Guy had given Bruges and replacing it with the earlier one that restored all Bruges' rights and privileges. He replied to Guy's objections by invading Flanders with an army of 60,000 men. Guy, without support of either the burghers or the wealthy elite, capitulated in October of 1297, agreeing to an armistice and a three-year truce.

"At the end of the truce, Philip again poured his troops into Flanders. Unable to defend the county and to end hostilities, Guy agreed to abandon the territory, submit himself to the king's mercy, and travel to Paris to face the monarch. He was promised that if peace did not occur within a year, he could return to Flanders.

"The king consulted his legal advisors, determined that Guy had forfeited his territory, threw him into prison, took possession of the region, and declared it annexed to France.

"French troops occupied Flanders and resentment among the general populace soared. They wanted King Philip's help with Guy, but not at the price of becoming subjects of France. The anxious burghers of Bruges were fearful that Philip would whittle away the hard won liberties and privileges of their town despite his earlier restoration of them. They had undermined the power and authority of their count and now found themselves in a far worse predicament. Only the French-sympathizing, wealthy elite were pleased with the development."

Guild Houses

Many of the shops along Steenstraat, off the Markt, were guild houses in medieval times. Starting at the Markt, proceed to Steenstraat. Steenstraat 19 was the bakers' guild house, Steenstraat 25 was the masons', Steenstraat 38, the joiners', Steenstraat 40 the cobblers'. Look for symbols of the craft on the buildings, sometimes on the façade, sometimes on the roof.

Return to the Markt. Several guild houses, now restaurants, may be seen here. Look for symbols atop the facades.

Take Wollestraat from the Markt. On the right, the Market Hall surrounds the belfry. The amazing growth of the weaving industry and cloth trade in the 13th through the 15th centuries made a communal warehouse and market essential. Here, merchants met their international clients and traded textiles, art and other products for wine, oil, spices, and a myriad of foreign goods. The major share of space was given to textiles. Lining the aisles on the ground floor were 384 stalls for displaying merchandise.

At 13 Wollestraat the former weaver's guild house boasts an elegant façade. For centuries, textile production was the backbone of Bruges' economy. Continue on Wollestraat to Dijver. Look along the canal to your left. You will see a beautiful turreted brick building framed by softly drooping trees along the canal. This is the tanners' guild house and one of the most photographed sites in Bruges.

Return to the Markt and take Philipstockstraat to Cordoeaniers Street. The guild house for diamond cutters is at #5.

Chapter Seven

"It sounds as though the city was politically split," I said.

"Yes, it was. The resentful and discontented Flemish party, the party of the masses, wanted independence. The upper class French party maintained allegiance to France. The elite of Bruges were almost evenly divided between those who were loyal to France and those who were loyal to Flanders. What happened next led to a great victory for Flemish morale.

"It started when Philip the Fair, King of France, accompanied by his queen, Jeanne of Navarre, triumphantly rode into Bruges in 1301. He was at last in control of the wealthy Flemish lands he had long coveted.

"Fawning magistrates and ostentatious displays greeted the royal pair. Gorgeous textiles draped palaces and public buildings. Wives and daughters of wealthy burghers attired in silks and satins with accessories of precious jewels stood on taffeta-draped balconies. Accustomed to seeing such displays of luxury only among the nobility, the queen caustically remarked that every woman of Bruges was her rival!

"City magistrates announced public games at the request of the king. Normally the common people participated with enthusiasm, but hostility to the monarch overrode their usual good humor and they flatly refused. Officials later tried to assign the cost of the elaborate uniforms, manufactured expressly for the games, to city companies. The companies, in turn, refused to accept the charges.

"Talk of revolt raced through the Flemish party.

"Soon after the king and his cortege left the city, Pieter de Coninc, dean of the weaver's guild and a man of considerable influence within the Flemish party, stood on a pedestal in the Markt and thundered against the corruption and ambition of the city fathers. The crowd cheered as he railed against the proposed assessment and urged the people to oppose it.

"The magistrates arrested and imprisoned de Coninc and his followers, but the people, furious with the officials' action, broke into the prison that night and released the prisoners. In the bloody revolt that followed, lives of several French sympathizers were lost.

"The rebellion was quickly put down by the arrival of French forces. The French commander, who took over the city, promptly revoked all the privileges of the town and levied an obnoxious tax. Against people who treasured their independence, despised taxation, and resented the French presence, these were disastrous moves.

"Fevered discontent roared through the city and on May 12, 1302, a deputation of Bruges burghers approached de Coninc and his band of followers who were now based in Damme. Convinced the French commander was planning a massacre of the entire city, they urged de Coninc help them strike the first blow.

"Led by de Coninc and Jan Breidel, a wealthy butcher who helped finance the revolt, the band of patriots burst into the city at dawn the next day. Shouting in Flemish a word that required a uniquely Flemish pronunciation, they slaughtered anyone who did not answer properly, a clever ploy since the French were incapable of pronouncing certain Flemish sounds. More than 1500 French and French sympathizers were massacred in what became known as the "Matins of Bruges."

"By June, the French king had amassed a formidable army and, led by the Count of Artois, invaded Flanders. French troops terrorized civilians as they entered Flemish speaking territories, adding to the outrage of the people.

"The Flemings assembled an army of resistance from throughout the countryside and from every Flemish city. Realizing their army was far smaller than the French army even with all the new recruits they devised a strategy to take their opponents by surprise. On July 11, 1302, the opposing forces faced each other.

"The land between the French and Flemish forces was marshy, with streams running through it in all directions. The Flemings, on foot and familiar with the countryside, had concealed the water with brushwood. The French, on horseback and unfamiliar with the terrain, were unaware of the dangerous conditions they were entering and attacked. Their horses, unable to swim through the brush, became ensnared in the scrubby cover, fell into the water, and drowned. The first two divisions were destroyed and the third, the reserve battalion, made a hasty, disorderly retreat."

"How clever," I exclaimed.

"Yes it was. Those ingenious Flemings had defeated the far more powerful army of a country that would have relegated them to servitude.

"The 'Battle of the Golden Spurs,' named for the 500 pairs of golden spurs taken from French aristocrats who died in the conflict, became a symbol of Flanders' struggle for independence and freedom.

"When you return to Bruges," said Anders, "take a look at the statues of Pieter de Coninc and Jan Breidel on the Markt."

"The triumph was a great victory for the Flemish spirit, but in terms of freedom from French domination, it was short lived. Military action continued through 1304. The Flemings won most of the skirmishes until August of that year when the French fleet defeated their army at Zierikzee.

A land battle followed with the French badly damaged, but with neither side the clear winner.

"The appearance of a new Flemish army in 1305 motivated the French to enter into peace negotiations. However, the terms exacted such heavy burdens on the Flemish, the cities refused to accept the treaty. Negotiations continued for 15 years amid constant upheaval and military action.

"In 1316, famine followed crop failure and Bruges lost almost 10 per cent of its population. Clergy preached to the peasants that a new era had arrived and they were the equals of aristocrats. In 1324 the peasants revolted against the aristocracy, a rebellion that lasted five years. Magistrates appointed by the count were expelled and nobles' castles burned.

"All the craft guilds and some of the city's patricians supported the uprising. In fact, the wealthy guildsmen, not the poor and oppressed, led the revolt. A weaver and fuller party gained control of the administration and dominated it toward the end of the rebellion.

"But why?" I asked.

"Because it was more than class conflict by the peasants. It was an effort by wealthy citizens to weaken the current ruling count, Louis of Male.

Yet nothing seemed to dim Bruges' economic exuberance, not even its endless political turmoil."

Damme

Board the bus "#4 St. Jozef Koolkerke" on the Markt square. The bus will take you to Noorweegse Kaai, the starting point for a boat trip to Damme on the river barge "Lamme Goedzak."

Pieter DeConinc and Jan Breidel

The bronze statue honoring the two heroes of the Matins of Bruges and the Battle of the Golden Spurs dominates the Markt square.

Belfry

Visit the treasury room in the belfry. Pass through the arch under the belfry and begin the climb to the tower. On the first level, you can purchase admission to the belfry and the treasury room.

The original belfry was built of wood and burned down in 1280, destroying the precious charter of the city that outlined its rights, privileges, and monopolies. Guy de Dampierre, the ruling count, subsequently refused to reinstate the charter and instead, instituted his own laws that sharply curtailed the city's ancient rights and liberties. Not until 1297 was the charter re-established.

The belfry was rebuilt of stone and a treasury room constructed for the safekeeping of the charter and the seal of the city. So precious did the people hold these documents, four wrought iron gates were created requiring 10 keys for opening. Eight different guild masters kept eight of the keys and two were in the hands of two separate city officials. The gates could not be opened without the presence of all ten men.

*You must climb **366** steps to reach the top of the belfry, If you are in condition, the ascent is well worth the effort. You* *will be rewarded with a magnificent panoramic view of the city and a chance to see the 47 bells of the carillon.*

Chapter Eight

"Did textiles continue to be the main export?" I asked.

"For a while, but it was the interaction of many events that continued the town's prosperity.

"In the 14th century, Bruges had become the most important city in Northern Europe, dominating international trade and finance. Bankers from Italy and merchants from the Rhine, Genoa, Castile, and the German and London Hanses thronged to the city and set up headquarters.

"To service this wealthy, cosmopolitan population, a fifth of the residents provided service as tailors, skilled craftsmen and utensil makers. A fourth of the populace were involved in the wholesale trades, the money market, or the hotel business. Entrepreneurs were assured of continuing income from tolls, brokerage fees and other commissions from monopolies granted by the count.

"To facilitate the buying and selling of merchandise, Bruges developed a sophisticated financial system that involved money changing, short and long term investments, letters of exchange and loans. The ease of making financial arrangements for doing business lubricated the wheels of commerce. Bankers, pawnbrokers, and moneychangers became important cogs in those wheels. Italian bankers, firmly established in the city by the end of the fourteenth century, controlled international finance entirely.

"Innkeeping, a flourishing trade that accommodated the influx of foreigners, often evolved into brokering services.

International traders who stayed in the inns needed space to store their merchandise and people who spoke the local language to act as intermediaries.

"The textile industry that peaked in the 13th century had begun a silent decline, however, noticeable mostly among those who dealt in cloth for foreign export. England and Holland had learned to weave their own fine cloth and produced it more cheaply than Bruges, undercutting international demand for the Flemish product.

"Still, a vigorous domestic market masked decreasing foreign demand. Orders from the upper classes and nobility kept the looms humming. Some weavers experimented with weaving tapestries, but enjoyed only moderate success.

"International trade in commodities other than textiles was brisk. Wool, sheepskin, lead, and tin were imported from England and Scotland and resold. Hides, wood, copper, dried and pickled fish, pitch, and potash came from the Baltic-German Hanse. France, the Rhine, and Italy brought wine. Oranges, lemons, leather, wool, iron ore and sugar came from the Iberian Peninsula while luxury products, spices and alum were imported from Italy.

"Attractive privileges given by city administrators to foreigners drew them to the city in droves and kept overall prosperity high. A German colony had been present since the 13th century and Spaniards received their first privileges during the early 14th century, exchanging saffron, oil, iron, nuts, and dried fruits both for locally produced goods and for products brought by other foreigners. The Spanish community made Bruges its permanent home and for centuries was an integral part of Bruges society.

"Although the English established a trading presence, English businessmen were transient, unlike the Germans, Italians, and Spaniards whose personnel often stayed for years. Perhaps the proximity of Flanders to England made coming and going relatively easy and permanent headquarters unnecessary.

"The Van der Beurse family operated a hotel on a square where bankers had their headquarters. The custom arose of merchants and bankers meeting daily in front of the hotel to establish monetary exchange rates. The square became known as the 'beursplein.' Evolving from this name is the term 'bourse,' meaning stock exchange. In 1279, the first stock exchange in history was established in Bruges."

"Bruges had become an exciting place," I said.

"Yes, the little Celtic settlement had become a wealthy, powerful city.

"The Flemish counts, however, to whom Bruges was supposed to be subject, had to tread carefully to maintain the peace and keep taxes rolling into their coffers.

"Count Louis of Nevers, in 1323, made a serious mistake by giving his relative, John of Namur, control over the Sluis waterways. This act violated Bruges' informal monopoly on goods entering the Zwin at Sluis and the fiercely protectionist Brugeans retaliated by imprisoning the count, burning the town, and taking John captive. To gain his freedom and restore peace, Louis was forced to replace Bruges' informal arrangement with an obligatory and exclusive monopoly.

"Sluis had become crucial to Bruges' economy. Foreign ships had to dock at Sluis before transferring their cargo to smaller vessels for navigating the shallower Zwin. The monopoly required most goods entering the Zwin at Sluis to be sold in Bruges. Without that guarantee, profits of the burghers would slide dangerously.

"New buildings rose in keeping with the town's wealth. In 1376 Count Louis of Male who succeeded his father, Louis of Nevers, laid the foundation stone for the magnificent gothic town hall, the first in Flanders. The building consisted of two stories lavishly decorated with carving and sculptures. The lower level contained offices and kitchens, the upper, a splendid aldermen's chamber embellished with wall paintings, sculptures and a huge, ornate fireplace. In 1379, Gilles de Man, a well-known painter, gilded the niches of the façade and in 1434-35, the great artist Jan van Eyck painted the statues that were placed in them. French revolutionaries destroyed the statues in the 18th century. Those currently in place were installed in the 20th century.

"More than 40,000 people now lived in the Center City. Picturesque walls, gates, and canals, soaring spires and towers and magnificent gothic architecture made the city a beautiful landmark. The emergence of a sizeable, prosperous middle class who could fill the city's coffers and afford luxurious town homes added to the growing splendor of the town.

"Bruges had grown rich and powerful, but not far beyond the palaces of the rich lay the hovels of the poor who did not participate in the economic boom. In 1349 an epidemic of plague raced through the city killing people by the hundreds, especially the poor.

"To alleviate some of the misery, the churches built almshouses for the poor and handicapped and several of the guilds developed small communities of almshouses for members who had come on hard times. Wealthy merchants added to the pool of cottages.

"At least there was some social consciousness," I said.

"Yes," he said. "At one time 80 developments housed the needy, but many of those were built in later centuries and were generally available only to the elderly, the physically disabled and those who had recently lost their livelihood. There was nothing for the chronically poor.

"Affluence did not remove the threat of conflict. With no centrally administered government, rivalry between cities posed recurring problems.

"Bruges and Ghent were traditional rivals and Louis of Male favored Bruges. When he allowed a canal to be built that would link the Leie River to the Bruges network on the

Zwin, tension gripped the competing cities. Fear grew among the people of Ghent that the new canal would divert trade from their own city.

"The burghers of Bruges did not want conflict with Ghent, but Ghent was determined to stop its rival's encroachment. While Gilles de Man painted the Town Hall niches, Ghent's rage swelled until the city erupted in rebellion and forced Louis into exile.

"Celebrations in Bruges have always been occasions for heavy drinking and merrymaking. In May of 1382, when the procession of the Holy Blood was being feted in Bruges, the Ghent militia took advantage of the people's widespread inebriation, defeated the Bruges militia and took possession of the town.

"Word of the revolt spread through French towns like sand in a sandstorm with French rebels crying for support of Ghent. The king of France, alarmed by the agitation in his own cities sent his army into Flanders to crush the rebellion.

"Men of Bruges and Ghent forgot their differences long enough to defend the territory but to little avail. The king's soldiers slaughtered the Flemish army at Westrozebeke and executed rebels, including 224 people in Bruges. The property of almost 300 was confiscated."

"It seems the French kings have regularly interfered in Flemish business," I said.

"Remember, in the feudal system, the Netherlands, and consequently, Flanders, was closely tied to France. Its rulers were vassals of the French king."

"Oh," I said. "What happened then?"

"When Louis died in 1384, Margaret, his daughter, succeeded her father. Fifteen years earlier, in 1369, she had married the French noble, Philip the Bold, Duke of Burgundy, who was the brother of King Charles V of France. With her ascension, a new era of rule by the dukes of Burgundy was ushered in and continued for almost a century.

"Philip the Bold made his "Joyous Entry" into Bruges in the year of Count Louis' death. He was installed as count in a solemn, traditional religious ceremony in Saint Donatian's and, although he made the customary promises to uphold traditions and privileges of the city, he visited Flanders only eight times during his 20 year tenure. As regent, his wife Margaret was the de facto ruler.

"During his reign, Louis of Male had removed many privileges of foreigners. Philip gradually restored the privileges with the single exception of those enjoyed by the English. Between 1386 and 1389, England, at war with France, was again the enemy.

"With a French duke as their ruler, Flemings were now constrained to side with the French in military conflicts. Flemish militias entered the war against England and English wool imports ceased altogether. However, Bruges merchants, never particularly loyal to their counts, openly negotiated with England for resumption of trading relations even as the count planned an invasion of that country.

"In 1396, official commerce with the English finally resumed and the rulers signed a 28-year truce that permitted English merchants to trade openly with Flemish cities. Once again the burghers were assured of a dependable supply of English wool."

"So peace came again?"

"Yes, but it still was not a happy period for Bruges.

"John the Fearless followed his father Philip in 1404 as the next Duke of Burgundy. To the great consternation of the Estates General, Flanders was once more faced with an absentee ruler. The Estates General was a decision-making body recognized by the count and made up of representatives from the three most important Flemish cities - Bruges, Ghent and Ypres.

"Duke John spent most of his time in France. Fearful their ruler's involvement in French politics would result in Flanders becoming the battlefield in another conflict between England and France, the Estates General begged him to become less involved in French politics, to stay home and to lead the Netherlands as a neutral state. John agreed, but nothing changed. Charles VI, King of France, was going mad and increasingly unable to lead his country. Power hungry John was eager to fill the gap being left. Unfortunately, his cousin, the Duke of Orleans, coveted the same role.

"In 1407, the Duke of Orleans, answering a summons to the king's presence, left the queen's palace at night with a small retinue of attendants. The duke had scarcely left the grounds when a band of armed men attacked and slashed him to death with their axes. A tall man with his face concealed by a hat rushed out from the palace, smashed a club into the Duke's head, and cut off his hand. Later in Paris, John the Fearless openly admitted his part in the vicious killing and immediately fled the city, hotly pursued. He escaped to Ghent where he tried to justify the crime to the Estates General.

"In consultation with Friar Petit of Paris, a divinity professor at the Sorbonne and a person well received at court, John concocted a rationalization for the murder that the friar, handsomely rewarded, carried back to the court.

"When John thought it safe, he returned to Paris and was greeted as a hero rather than a rogue. At a solemn assembly, he affirmed all that Friar Petit had circulated. The deed was done, he said, with a view to the king's safety, to preserve the monarch's line, and for the welfare of the realm. Scribes recorded his laudable motives and the lie echoed throughout France. The king accepted his spurious explanation and rewarded rather than punished him for his evil deed.

"Outraged, the Orleanists vowed to avenge the murder of their duke. Twelve years later, in September of 1419, John was slain by the dauphin of France, now head of the Orleanist party, on a bridge over the Seine. Whether it was self-defense, as the dauphin claimed, or murder will never be known."

City Hall

Return to the Burg. On the first floor of the gothic city hall is the impressive Gothic Hall. Note the wooden and polychromed vaulted ceiling. The murals covering the walls depict events important in the history of Bruges.

Europe in Bruges

From the Burg, take Burgstraat to Philipstockstraat, turn left, and continue on Philipstockstraat to Vlamingstraat. Turn right on Vlamingstraat. The Genoese Lodge built in 1399 and now a cultural center, is at 33 Vlamingstraat. Note the relief of Saint Elizabeth and Saint George on the façade. Next door at #35 is the Van der Beurse House, originally built in 1276, where merchants and bankers met in the 13th and 14th centuries to establish foreign exchange rates. The term "bourse" for stock exchange evolved from the name of the family who operated the famous inn.

Proceed along Vlamingstraat to Academiestraat. Turn right on Academiestraat. Number 1 Academiestraat was the headquarters of the Florentine merchants from 1420.

Continue along Academiestraat. To the left is Spanjaardstraat, center of the Spanish community. At #18 Academiestraat is the Burghers' Lodge where wealthy burghers and foreign merchants met for social functions. Straight ahead is the statue of Jan van Eyck on Jan van Eyck Square (Jan van Eyckplein). At #2 Jan van Eyckplein is a handsome house with a red door and the shield of the Luxembourg's. This was the medieval tollhouse where ships had to pay taxes on goods brought into the city by boats from the outports of Damme and Sluis. The canal that served the tollhouse has been filled in.

Veer left at Genthof and left again at Woensdagmarkt. In the center of the square is a statue of the master painter, Hans Memling. Continue through the square to Krom Genthof, the first street on the right. At #1 is the Oosterlinghuis, the Easterling House, headquarters of the Hanseatic League whose presence in the city dated from the 13th century. The house was given to the League as part of a package of concessions to encourage their return after leaving the city for the third time in 1451. The building originally had an imposing tower and was twice as high as the present structure.

Return to Genthof. At #7 you will see one of two surviving wooden houses from the 15th century.

To retrace your steps to the Markt: Turn right on Academiestraat to Vlamingstraat, left on Vlamingstraat to the Markt square. Cross the square to Breidelstraat. Enter Breidelstraat and immediately begin looking for a narrow walkway on the right called De Garre. De Garre is typical of lanes that provided access to canals for fire control. Turn right into the lane and look for the De Garre tavern. Take time to enjoy two or three of the 130 marvelous Belgian beers served there.

Social Consciousness

Godshuizen (almshouses) were founded to help the elderly, the handicapped and the needy, but not the chronically poor. The earliest were established in 1303. At one time 80 compounds were present in the city. Today the 47 that remain have been modernized and are occupied by the elderly. Each complex has its own private garden and chapel. Residents live free of charge and maintenance is provided by the city. When the houses were built, the only requirement for residence, other than poverty, was that prayers be said for those who built them. Below is a sample of those that remain.

To get there from the Markt: <u>De Vos Almshouse</u> (1713). Take Wollestraat to Dijver, turn right, and proceed to Mariastraat. Turn left on Mariastraat and continue to Wijngaardstraat. Turn right and continue to Noordstraat. The almshouse is at Noordstraat 2-8.

<u>Rooms Couvent</u> (1330). Katelijnstraat 9-10. Katelijnstraat is a continuation of Mariastraat. From the De Vos Almshouse, return to Mariastraat. Turn right.

<u>Hertsberge Almshouse</u> (ca 1335). 87-101 Katelijnstraat.

<u>Saint Jozef and Meulenaere Almshouses.</u> Return toward Mariastraat. Watch for Nieuwe Gentweg on your right. Since the Diamond Museum is on the corner, you may want to go through the museum before continuing. The museum displays a fascinating history of Bruges as well as of the city's diamond cutting and diamond trade.

Continue on Nieuwe Gentweg to the row of white almshouses with black trim and shutters. They are to the right on Nieuwe Gentweg. If the entry is not locked, go into the formal garden for a few moments of silence and meditation.

Chapter Nine

"Did Philip the Good follow his father, John the Fearless, as the next Burgundian count? I asked.

"Yes, but in the early years of his reign, he was far from good. He was brilliant and he was a tyrant. His rule started well enough for Bruges, but later, when he ignored the protectiveness of his subjects for their historic rights and privileges, a horrendous conflict ensued. This is how it came about.

"Prior to John's murder, the dukes of Burgundy had been enemies of England. John's death produced a dramatic shift in loyalties. Grieving his father's violent death and wanting vengeance against the French crown, Duke Philip abandoned the Netherlands' historic relationship with France and openly entered into a compact with Henry IV, king of England. The alliance remained in place for 16 years.

"Those years were good for Bruges. Trade across the channel went on without interruption, to the city's great benefit.

"Philip also spent more time in Bruges than any of his predecessors with the Prinsenhof as his base. Festivities, processions, and tournaments charged the city with excitement. The Court thrilled the people with its luxury.

"Burgundian dukes were known to be fond of displaying their riches. Between 1405 and 1482 they sponsored no less than 24 tournaments involving jousts and combat that each lasted 10 to 15 days. The chief purpose of the tournaments was to encourage support for the dukes' policies, a successful strategy for the most part.

"Philip's marriage to Isabella of Portugal in 1430 brought pomp and ceremony to new heights. Her entourage of fourteen ships reached Sluis on Christmas Day, but, delayed by seasickness, the princess did not arrive in Bruges until shortly after New Year's Day.

"Leaders of 52 guilds and foreign merchants representing thirty-four nations accompanied nearly 150 officials of Bruges to welcome her at the Damme Gate. A crowd in the thousands lined her way into the city where she was met by the duke and his retinue of hundreds.

"To celebrate his marriage, Philip created the Order of the Golden Fleece, an elite brotherhood available only to members of the highest nobility. Knighthood conferred on admission to the Order was the most prestigious recognition given by the Burgundian court and bound the count's great nobles in a personal oath to the house of Burgundy. From that time on, the Knights of the Golden Fleece figured prominently in jousts and tournaments.

"Louis van Gruuthuse, one of its most illustrious members, was admitted to the Order in 1461. A loyal vassal of Burgundian dukes and a skilled diplomat, he was instrumental in keeping Bruges out of the rebellion of Ghent in 1452. He would later cool the tempers of his fellow citizens in negotiations with Philip's granddaughter, Mary of Burgundy, after the unexpected death in 1477 of her father, Charles the Bold.

"The knights met three times in Bruges in the 15th century: at Saint Donatian's, at Our Lady's and at Saint Savior's. A painted panel bearing the coat of arms of each knight hung above the choir stall where they sat for the meeting. Those in Saint Savior's and Our Lady's are in place today as they were in the 15th century.

"This all sounds pretty good to me. Where was the tyranny?" I asked.

"It was good at first, but it wouldn't last," he replied. "As Philip became involved in domestic affairs, trouble erupted. He was convinced a centralized power structure would give him greater control over his Flemish subjects. His initial strategy was to weaken the positions of the three big cities, Bruges, Ghent, and Ypres.

"During the reign of earlier Burgundian dukes the people conditioned support for their counts' wars and luxurious lifestyles on the award of privileges and concessions. Consequently, the citizens of Bruges were now freer and more independent than at any time in their history and were unwilling to give an inch to Philip. They violently opposed his centralizing moves, seeing centralization as a threat to their autonomy and monopolies.

"Even more serious for Bruges, relations with England had become shaky during the preceding five years. Henry VI's regents could not hold back the French from recovering the northern part of the Netherlands.

"To protect his domain, Philip settled his differences with the French crown by signing the Treaty of Arras in 1435. Conditions of the treaty forced the king of France to renounce all feudal rights over Philip personally and to give him the Somme towns as his southern boundary. This was good for Philip, but terrible for Bruges. Once more Flanders and England were enemies, a disastrous situation for Bruges since, as we know, the city depended on English wool for textile production.

"When England suspended wool exports, dissatisfaction with Philip reached a new high. The English monarch, enraged by Philip's defection, withheld trade from the territory until 1439. The textile industry crumbled under the blow.

"England attacked Flanders at Calais. The count needed the support of Bruges, Ghent, and Ypres to defend the territory, but the citizens of Bruges, angered by their loss of trade, gave only half-hearted support. The burghers who answered his call to military service served only two months. When the Burgundian fleet fled before the English admiral, the men of Bruges stationed at Calais packed up and went home.

"Bruges had enjoyed monopolistic privileges over its outport of Sluis since Louis of Male granted them in 1323. Over time, violations eroded the city's hold on the port to such an extent that by the time of Philip's war with England, Bruges had lost much of its control, a source of great frustration and loss of income to the burghers.

"In 1436, bringing an order signed by Isabella, Duchess of Burgundy, Bruges burghers sent an armed force to Sluis, ostensibly to defend the port against the English but with the true purpose of reclaiming their rights to the city. Based on Bruges' 14th century legal jurisdiction, they demanded the town and its fleet be turned over to them.

"The angry people of Sluis threw the Brugeans out of their town even though both Sluis and Bruges were supposedly allies in the struggle against England. No attention whatever was paid to the official order. Rioting followed and in the fray, both Ghent and the Franc of Bruges came to the assistance of Bruges. Hostility was so extreme, Duchess Isabella fled to Ghent.

"Duke Philip was furious about the conflict, but unable to withstand the united pressure of Bruges, Ghent and the Franc, he acknowledged Bruges' historical rights, punished the officials of Sluis and said he would shortly arrive in Damme to redress the grievances of the Brugeans. First, he insisted, they must disarm.

"The men returned to their homes, put away their weapons and awaited their ruler's arrival. They waited - and waited. After four days with no word from Philip, they realized they had been duped; he did not intend to keep his word. When they learned he was augmenting his forces with troops from Lille and Holland, they were stunned by the betrayal and prepared for battle. The Markt filled with the men of Bruges and those of 62 neighboring villages armed and ready to fight.

"Foreign merchants, in an effort to prevent damage to trade, approached the count in Damme and urged him to resume negotiations. At first, he adamantly refused, but finally, under pressure of their threats, he relented.

"The merchants returned to Bruges and the city officials agreed to meet with the count. The burghers, distrusting their ruler, detained his ambassadors in Bruges until their own returned. The meeting was held, they agreed on terms, Philip confirmed the city's rights and privileges, and an uneasy peace followed. An undercurrent of grumbling persisted on both sides.

"Still determined to weaken the power of Bruges, the duke granted a charter to the Franc of Bruges, creating a fourth member of the Estates General. Under its provisions, freeholders in the Franc were forbidden to become burghers of the city. Since Bruges had a substantial number of burghers who lived outside the city, probably important for the military service they were obligated to provide and for the taxes they paid, the duke's action sparked outrage. The grumbling, no longer subdued, reached crisis proportions. The aldermen and the mayor were helpless to contain the riots that erupted. In the melee, the mayor lost his life.

"When the storm cleared and tempers had cooled, the burghers, fearful for the consequences of their hot-headedness, sent a delegation to the count with excuses and explanations for their actions. The count was not impressed, but condescended to pass through Bruges on his way to Holland.

"Three months later he arrived with a large contingent of soldiers and knights and sent word to the new mayor of Bruges that his men would camp at Male. He would enter with only a handful of attendants.

"Next morning as Philip approached the city, the new mayor went out to welcome the ruler. However, the count was not accompanied by a small contingent, but by an armed guard of 2000. The mayor's furious arguments had little effect. The troops marched on the city and some of the knights reached the Zand before the alarm could be sounded. When at last it rang, the town exploded with men swarming through the streets in such numbers and with such threatening demeanors, Philip quickly ordered his men to withdraw the way they had come.

"When he and his men reached the city gate they found it locked. They were trapped. Angry burghers attacked and killed several of the count's bodyguards and one of his most trusted captains. Philip escaped only by the misplaced loyalty of the softhearted mayor. Unable to calm the rioters, the official procured a smith to break open the lock of one of the gates and Philip rushed out with a handful of knights.

"The count blockaded Bruges and gave Sluis its commercial privileges. Nine months of warfare followed and foreign merchants fled to friendlier cities. The countryside surrounding Bruges was devastated and famine trailed close behind. Cold, plague and poverty racked the city.

"The people of Bruges appealed to their leaders to make peace at any price. Early in February of 1438, representatives of the city appeared before the count, begging for an end to hostilities.

"Philip, repulsed by the peoples' stubborn rebelliousness, cynically required all the city officials to appear before him outside the city gates, to beg on their knees for mercy, to offer to him all their goods as well as their persons and to present to him the keys to the city. He then publicly executed ten persons and levied a staggering fine that crippled the reeling city.

"Ironically, the mayor who risked his own life to help Philip escape was among those condemned to death. His wife and son also received death sentences, but the count commuted the punishment of the mayor to life imprisonment with torture and that of his wife to life imprisonment. In anguish, they watched their son's execution.

"The count's vengeance extended to the countryside as well as to the city and all kinds of rumors flew about. Acts of retribution and bloodshed were expected momentarily. Some citizens, determined to leave, hid their purpose saying they were going on pilgrimages to religious shrines. When their true intent was leaked, they were arrested and executed.

"Trade could not flourish in a climate of fear and betrayal. Foreign merchants who had returned after the declaration of peace threatened to leave en masse unless the count's harassment stopped. They demanded peace be entered into with England and commercial intercourse with that country re-established.

"In a serious blow to Bruges, the Hanseatic League, a powerful organization of merchants from free Germanic cities, left the city and established its headquarters in Antwerp.

"The threats of the foreign merchants and the departure of the Hanse brought the count to his senses. Satisfied he had humiliated the leaders of Bruges and humbled the city with outrageous fines, but mindful loss of revenue would follow an exodus of the merchants, Philip finally embarked upon a policy of peace.

"Peace was restored following the successful conclusion of a truce with England. Little by little, confidence and prosperity returned to the devastated city."

The Prinsenhof

From the Markt, enter Sint Jacobsstraat. Turn left at Geldmundstraat and right at Prinsenhof, three blocks from the beginning of Gelmundstraat. Now a convent, little remains of the original

Prinsenshof (1396) which occupied several city blocks in the 14th and 15th centuries.

Saint Savior's Cathedral

If you have not yet visited Saint Savior's Cathedral to see the escutcheons of the Knights of the Golden Fleece, return to Gelmundstraat and cross onto Kopstraat, go past Zilverstraat onto Kemelstraat to Steenstraat. Turn right. Saint Savior's is one block to your right.

The Zand

The Zand, where tournaments and jousts were held, is two blocks to the left as you exit Saint Savior's.

Chapter Ten

"So Philip the Tyrant tamed the burghers of Bruges. Did the peace last? "

"Yes, for as long as he lived. He not only subdued his defiant subjects, he began a reign that brought 29 years of peace and created the most dazzling period in Bruges' history.

"Two years after his confrontation with civic officials, Philip, Duke of Burgundy, Count of Flanders, made his triumphal entry into the town accompanied by the blare of trumpets and clanging of bells. The people, now docile and submissive, received him with enthusiastic ovations and demonstrations of goodwill. They adorned their houses and public buildings with fine tapestries and strewed flowers along his path. They even set up allegorical groups along his procession that symbolized repentance and submission. They had become as compliant and subservient as they had been hostile and defiant and now deferred to him as if he were a savior rather than the oppressor who had crushed them and brought them to their knees.

"Perhaps their memories were short, or perhaps the humiliation they had suffered was too fresh to risk further mortification. Until the end of his reign in 1467, the people's tractability was rewarded with the longest period without conflict in the city's history.

"Peace brought a superb environment. Music, poetry, art, and intellectual activity flourished. An ardent bibliophile with excellent taste, Philip acquired a library of more than

900 illuminated manuscripts during his rule. He and his court were patrons of the arts and the arts prospered during his regime.

"Bruges became the favorite residence of the duke and the presence of the court, with its magnificent festivities, colorful tournaments, and royal pageants gave the city renewed vitality. Sumptuous palaces were built and sanctuaries enlarged and adorned with art treasures.

"The presence of the court established an aristocratic tradition that was to distinguish the city for decades. In the court of Burgundy, good manners, courtesy, and encouragement of the arts were considered essential qualities of a civilized society and the refined ambience spilled over into the city. Bruges became known as a place where one could enjoy the 'good life.'

"Works of art were commissioned by the duke and members of his court, by the wealthy elite and by the higher clergy. In 1436, Jan Van Eyck created a magnificent altarpiece for Canon Joris Van der Paele of Saint Donatian's Church for the Canon's tomb in the cathedral. The masterpiece now hangs in the Groeninge Museum.

"Did painters have to join a guild?" I asked.

"As a rule, they found it in their interests to join the prominent and powerful painter's guild, but a few, such as Jan van Eyck and Hans Memling, worked directly with their patrons.

"Van Eyck was the first and greatest of the artists known as the Flemish Primitives," continued Anders. "He set a standard for art that is still unsurpassed more than 500 years later. One of his signal achievements was the rediscovery and refinement of the ancient art of oil painting. Using thin pigmented oil glazes and varnishes, laboriously applied layer upon layer, he achieved a translucent, enamel-like surface with colors so luminous and clear they appear today as they did in the 15th century."

"What do you mean by 'Flemish Primitives?' Are their works crude?"

The chair shook with his laughter. "Far from it. *Primitief* doesn't translate well into English. A better definition would be 'early Flemish master painters.' Their work was beautiful and highly refined, as you will see when you visit the Groeninge Museum.

"Van Eyck was an interesting man. Not only was he in the employ of the duke as an artist, he was also a trusted diplomat. On more than one occasion, the duke sent him on secret missions to foreign countries where he used painting as a cover for his actual purpose. Before agreeing to marry Isabella of Portugal, Philip dispatched Van Eyck to Portugal with orders to paint her portrait so that he might see what she looked like.

"The long period of peace gave middle class citizens as well as nobility and the wealthy time and funds to patronize the arts. Hans Memling, a master portrait painter, received commissions from churchmen, Italian bankers, townspeople, and the monks and nuns of Saint John's Hospital. The four leaders in charge of Saint John's commissioned his magnificent triptych of Saint John. The hospital community commissioned the Saint Ursula shrine, a wooden chest in the shape of a gothic chapel beautifully painted to tell the story of Saint Ursula and the 11,000 virgins martyred at Cologne. The superb collection of Memling's works hanging in the Memling Museum of Saint John's Hospital also includes the awe-inspiring 'Mystic Marriage of Saint Catherine'."

"Philip instituted economic policies that stimulated the expansion of trade and created a period of political and monetary stability that led to unprecedented affluence. Foreign merchants returned, trade flourished, and some local merchants amassed great fortunes. Flanders had been a debt-ridden province when Philip took it over, but by the end of his sovereignty the county, and Bruges in particular, had made him the richest ruler in Europe.

The old man stood and stretched, then sank into his over-stuffed chair again.

"We can stop any time and continue another day," I said.

"No, I'm fine. Let's continue. We're on the verge of some huge changes in the city.

"Bruges had the outward show of a fabulously wealthy city. However, international commerce was beginning to wane. The luxury of the court and the city's booming domestic market masked an insidious erosion of income from services that supported international traders.

"Although a significant number of foreign traders remained in Bruges, an increasing number plied their trade elsewhere. The Hanseatic League had returned after peace was restored, but left again from 1451-1457 following a dispute with the count. The league established its headquarters in Antwerp, a serious blow to Bruges. Amsterdam and Antwerp were growing in importance, posing a challenge to Bruges' dominance over the international market.

"Nevertheless, the city retained its place in European commercial activity throughout much of the 15th century by shifting the emphasis away from the production of fine textiles and other traditional goods to the production of luxury items. Miniature art, Flemish primitive panel painting, and book printing became popular. The diamond trade and production of armaments became a source of income as well. As the textile market declined, tapestry weaving grew in popularity. However, the need for banks, tolls, and other commercial facilities that generated the major portion of foreign capital diminished. Innkeepers, moneychangers, and commercial brokers were less in demand as foreign traders left. Disappearance of "soft" sources of wealth would eventually prove a fateful problem.

"The constant silting of the Zwin continued to threaten Bruges' vital link to the sea. Ships still docked at the port city of Sluis and transferred their cargoes to smaller vessels for transport into the city, but navigation of the passage was becoming more difficult.

"The city's treasury became emptier, relief rolls grew longer and included not only the chronically poor, but clergy, merchants, and respected people whose families had been citizens of Bruges for centuries.

"Adding to the mounting problems, city leaders pursued protectionist policies that suppressed the rural areas on which they had to rely for food and raw materials even as the guilds created more and more regulations trying to stem the tide of economic change. Brilliant on its surface, decay was spreading like a hidden cancer."

"In 1467, Philip suffered a fatal stroke. He was buried in Saint Donatian's and bitterly mourned. The people remembered only the years of peace and prosperity under his later rule. He had succeeded in making himself beloved and went down in history not as Philip the Tyrant, but as Philip the Good."

Groeninge Museum

To get there from the Burg: Enter Blinde Ezelstraat, proceed to Rozenhoedkaai, bear right. The museum is approximately four blocks straight ahead and across the street at #12 Dijver.

To visualize the powerful count who tamed the burghers of Bruges and led the city into a period of unparalleled brilliance, visit the Groeninge Museum and view Philip the

Good's portrait painted by Roger Van der Weyden, Van Eyck's most famous student. The museum houses a magnificent collection of art from different periods. For this visit, you may want to focus on the Flemish Primitives and paintings by 15th century masters. Van Eyck's masterpiece, "The Virgin with the Canon Joris Van der Paele" created in 1441, is exquisite. Can you see the reflection of the virgin in the helmet of the soldier standing behind the Canon? Note the intimate details in the faces, the expressions of feeling, and the poor state of health of the Canon.

Be sure to view the painting of Louis van Gruuthuse by a 15th century master painter.

Gruuthuse Museum

The Gruuthuse palace at # 17 Dijver was one of the finest and largest in the city. The Gruuthuse family amassed great wealth through the sale of herbs that flavored beer. Louis' motto "Plus est en vous" (there is more to you than meets the eye) is in evidence throughout the mansion. The museum contains artifacts that give a sense of the daily life of wealthy 15th century Brugeans. If this is your first visit to the museum, take time to go through the kitchen and other rooms to observe the exhibits of lace, coins, tapestries, musical instruments, weapons, and furniture. Be sure to visit the oratory that connects the palace with the Church of Our Lady next door and permits a view of the choir and tombs of Mary of Burgundy and Charles the Bold. Its construction required special permission from the Pope.

During the 19th century restoration, the skeleton of a man was discovered in a secret chamber of the enormous kitchen fireplace. Behind the fireplace, a staircase led to two underground passages that branched in opposite directions.

Neither their destinations nor their purposes have been established.

Church of Our Lady

Countless treasures that enrich the interior of this lovely old church include works by Jan van Eyck, Gerard David, and Isenbrant. Escutcheons with the coats of arms of the Knights of the Golden Fleece, placed in the 15th century for a meeting of the Knights, hang above the choir stalls. Take time to absorb the beauty of Michelangelo's great sculpture of the Virgin and Child, said to be his only work to leave Italy during his lifetime. Originally built in the 9th century, the church was reconstructed and expanded in the 13th, 14th, 15th and 16th centuries.

Memling Museum in Saint John's Hospital

The Memling collection, housed in the church adjacent to Saint John's Hospital at #38 Mariastraat, contains several 15th century paintings by the brilliant artist, Hans Memling who dominated the artistic scene in Bruges for 30 years. Saint John's is across the street from the Church of Our Lady on Mariastraat.

Chapter Eleven

"Did the city go into a downward spiral after Philip died?" I asked.

"No, Bruges continued to have the appearance of a splendid, wealthy center of commerce and culture under his son, Charles the Bold. The people welcomed Charles' accession with enthusiasm, anticipating a continuance of his father's peaceful governance.

"Three months after coming to power, Charles allied himself with England by marrying the sister of King Edward IV.

"When he brought his English bride, Margaret of York, to Bruges, the lavish celebration exceeded even that of his father's marriage to Isabella. Charles decreed that a contest of the Golden Tree should be held in honor of his marriage and employed the master painter, Hugo Van der Goes, to decorate the town with dozens of golden trees in preparation for the event.

"Three hundred men were kept at work in the count's kitchen. Banquet tables groaned with edible ships, castles, and trees that symbolized the towns, duchies, and abbeys of the count's domain. Seven huge mirrors mounted on the walls magnified the display a thousandfold. Wine instead of water cascaded from fountains for the ten days of festivities.

"The opulent bridal procession, preceded by the blare of trumpets and the *clip-clop* of horses' hooves, astounded the people. Princess Margaret, as befit her lofty station, regally passed along the crowds that lined the streets wearing an exquisite gown of white and gold. Thirteen white horses decked with red and gold cloth and bearing thirteen young women dressed in fur-lined velvet cloaks followed her carriage. The main officials came next, garbed in black satin, the knights in black velvet, and the servers in simple black woolen clothing. The Duke was extravagantly robed in gold cloth with wide, slashed sleeves lined with marten.

"In a rainbow of colors, the parade of nations followed: Venetians in crimson velvet, Spaniards wearing purple damask, and Florentines in black satin robes riding horses decked out in white satin coverlets trimmed in blue velvet. Then proceeded the guilds, the clergy, and the city magistrates.

"Unfortunately, the people would soon learn their new count lacked his father's patience, political astuteness, and good business sense. The delight with which the people had greeted his accession faded as they realized he possessed none of the qualities that had made the city great under the rule of Philip the Good.

"Charles vehemently opposed the growing power of the French king, Louis XI. He settled into his role with fantasies of freeing himself from political dependence on France although fulfillment of the dream would mean war, conscription, and taxes for his subjects.

"Charles proceeded to burden the citizens of Bruges and the rest of Flanders with terrible taxes to support his wars. Even as Bruges was losing its place in international trade to Antwerp, taxes that were triple the average of the prior 15 years disheartened the people. A general feeling of uneasiness pervaded the town and again an undercurrent of grumbling reflected general disenchantment. While his father had made himself beloved, Charles estranged himself from his people.

"On January 5, 1477, during the defeat of the Burgundian army at Nancy, the count mysteriously disappeared. Rumors that he had been killed in battle flew about although his remains were never positively identified.

"Upon word of his disappearance, a riot broke out in Bruges. The people demanded that Charles' daughter and successor, Mary, redress their grievances. Although she was only nineteen years old and had little experience or power, Mary tried valiantly, with the aid of her ministers, to contain the discontent with political concessions. She granted a new charter that returned to Bruges the traditional liberties and commercial monopolies that had been taken away under Philip the Good, but her efforts to calm her subjects were only partially successful.

"Meanwhile, Louis XI of France looked hungrily at the wealth of the Low Countries and quickly absorbed the Duchy of Burgundy into his kingdom. Intent on reclaiming his fief, he invaded Flanders. With a 19-year-old girl at the helm, he was convinced the territory would be his. He had only to pressure her into marrying the dauphin, his son.

"To Mary, an alliance with France was unthinkable. She knew she must protect her domain from incursions by the French crown if the freedom and independence so precious to her subjects were to be preserved. Alone, she could not do it. She needed the backing of an empire as powerful as France.

"Frederick III, Emperor of the Holy Roman Empire, had a son of marriageable age. Before his death, Charles the Bold had made an agreement with Frederick for Mary to wed the emperor's son, Maximilian. Now, with the crisis produced by her father's death, arrangements were hurriedly made for the marriage to take place. An alliance with the Habsburgs and the backing of the German army would be a powerful deterrent to France. To speed the alliance, the couple were wed by proxy. Four months later a formal ceremony conferred the Church's blessing.

"Maximilian was only 18 years old at the time they exchanged vows and so short of funds Flanders was obliged to lend him money for travel expenses. Yet his young bride willingly turned over the governance of Flanders to her teenage husband."

"Was this the same man who became Maximilian I, Emperor of the Holy Roman Empire?" I asked.

"Yes, it was. But as a young, inexperienced ruler, he was a grave disappointment. He succeeded in infuriating and estranging the people who could have made him rich.

"He proved a weak, vain, vacillating ruler, unable to keep his word and with ambitions that exhausted his wife's treasury and emptied the city's. The burghers, at first enthusiastically loyal to the new count in the hope of returning to the stable policies of Philip the Good, had their hopes dashed once more. While the hard-working, thrifty citizens contributed to the cost of his war with France, Maximilian lavished expensive gifts on foreign favorites and sold many works from the famous library of the dukes of Burgundy. On one occasion, he put up Mary's jewels as security for loans from Spanish merchants to be repaid at usurious interest rates.

"His vacillation, ambition and profligacy became a source of great irritation and instead of receiving the people's support he became the object of their animosity. The economic stability established by Philip the Good and upon which the continuing prosperity of the city depended, was in shambles.

"The presence of Mary, a gentle woman loved by her people, probably kept the town from open rebellion against her husband. She was often seen walking along the street as any ordinary citizen, talking with the common people, her attire modest, her manner unassuming. She delighted in mixing with the people like any ordinary wife.

"In 1482, while hunting, her horse reared unexpectedly, lost its balance, and fell, crushing the young countess. She lingered for three weeks, but finally succumbed in her room in the Prinsenhof, leaving a three-year old son as heir.

"Maximilian called a meeting of the Estates General to persuade them to recognize him as Regent of Flanders and guardian of his son. The representatives refused although Mary, in her will, had given that right to her husband. Instead, the Estates appointed a Council of Regents. The council, comprised of relatives of Maximilian and Mary as well as representatives from Bruges, Ghent, Ypres, and the Franc of Bruges, governed Flanders until June of 1485.

"Maximilian did not give up easily, however. Conflict and war with the Habsburg prince followed, until finally, the weary people of Bruges and the other principal cities of Flanders agreed to his regency and allowed him the guardianship of his son.

"He brutally executed leaders who had opposed him with the exception of Louis van Gruuthuse. Gruuthuse, one of the wealthiest and most respected merchants of Bruges, was fined and sent to prison.

"During the next three years Maximilian made agreements with the cities, then arbitrarily retracted them, creating a climate of profound distrust. In 1487, when he entered Bruges with a German contingent, suspicion and resentment peaked. In this caustic atmosphere, he foolishly asked the city magistrates for money and soldiers to defend the borders of his territories.

"The peoples' anger reached a climax some months later when Maximilian tried to leave the city. A band of merchants and burghers took to the streets, imprisoned the count, and executed the Germans as well as anyone thought to side with them.

"To assure he would witness the punishment of his sympathizers, Maximilian was incarcerated in the Craenenberg, a mansion on the Markt belonging to a wealthy merchant.

"The burghers, hoping for compromise, even employed the artist Gerard David to paint over the bars on the windows so the ruler would be less aware of his confinement. City fathers surrounded him with a dozen attendants who looked to his every need, making him seem more guest than prisoner. The attendants, however, were also his jailers, charged with preventing his escape.

"Two weeks later Maximilian was transferred to another, more secure, palace where he remained for an additional nine weeks.

"Emperor Frederick III could not permit this outrageous treatment of his son and heir. He approached the city with his German army and, although he did not attack, the threat prompted the start of serious negotiations between the city and the count.

"Agreement was reached and Maximilian was released. With his treacherous history, it was amazing that city officials would believe Maximilian capable of honoring any accord or that he would fail to punish those who had dared imprison him.

"His retaliation was swift. From a safe distance, he issued a proclamation to all of Flanders that the agreement was made under duress and that he was not bound by it.

"Once more the people had been deceived and once more they took up arms against him, but it was a hopeless war. The strength and resources of his father's empire backed the deceitful young ruler.

"Bruges held out until 1490. In the meantime, the country around the city was ravaged. The dikes gave way, flooding the countryside. Very little food came into the city. Even some of the rich were starving. Trade was at a standstill and foreign merchants, discouraged by the constant strife that enveloped the city, relocated to Antwerp.

"With the exit of the merchants, demand for banking, brokering and money-changing services diminished to a trickle. The clamor for goods and services created by the presence of the Burgundian court evaporated and extensive unemployment paralyzed the city. By 1494, four to five thousand houses stood empty.

"When hostilities ceased, some of the foreign traders returned, but Bruges had been badly damaged by Maximilian. The city would never again achieve the position, prestige and prosperity of the 13th to 15th centuries."

"I thought the silting of the Zwin had caused Bruges' decline, but it seems Maximilian played a hefty part as well."

"That's right," said Anders. "The Zwin had been kept open for centuries by periodic dredging. Had the town remained at peace and economically stable, that process might have continued. Of course, with the competition of Antwerp and Amsterdam, changes were occurring, but Maximilian's betrayal was a major factor in the destruction of the city's economy."

The Craenenberg

Now a restaurant, all that remains of the original house where Maximilian was imprisoned is a sidewall. Have lunch here and try to imagine the frustration and fury of a ruler imprisoned by his subjects on a square where the execution of his German contingent was in full view.

Tombs of Charles the Bold and Mary of Burgundy

These magnificent tombs, adorned with life size carvings of the rulers, rest in the Church of Our Lady on Dijver and Mariastraat.

Chapter Twelve

"I suppose Bruges was now in serious decline," I said.

"It would appear so," said Anders, frowning, "but the city's decline was more like an undulation with a downward drift. Under Maximilian, the city reached a trench in the undulating pattern, then began to come up again.

"Maximilian's son, Philip I, took over the rule of Flanders in 1494 after Maximilian succeeded Frederick III as Emperor of the Habsburg Empire (the Holy Roman Empire). The peoples' spirit returned when they saw that at last they had a sensible ruler with their interests at heart. An excellent diplomat, he softened the demands of those who advocated centralizing the government and pacified the ones who favored regional independence. He restored the confidence of the Flemings when he re-established trading relations with England and released Anglo-Flemish trade from rules that were crippling it.

"Philip appointed his sister Margaret of Austria regent of the Netherlands. Also a fine politician, she governed the Low Countries in the early 1500's for Philip and later, for his son, Charles V. Under her non-aggressive rule, a peaceful, fairly prosperous period occurred and Bruges began to recover from the years of fighting Maximilian. The city did not attain its former brilliance, but it was still a center of patronage of the arts and encouragement of intellectual pursuits. In spite of civic tumult and loss of its former place in international trade,

Bruges' magnetism for artists did not weaken and they continued to create great works.

"The old, rich families residing in the city, less affected by the turmoil under Maximilian, patronized the artists and scholars. In 1506, through the prominent Mouscroun family, Michelangelo's magnificent statue of the Virgin and Child was brought from Italy to Bruges and installed in Our Lady's Church.

"Gerard David, admitted to the painter's guild of Bruges in 1484, had become a wealthy, prominent citizen by 1521. David created the 'Baptism of Christ,' a modest triptych, and the horrifying 'Judgment of Cambyses,' a representation of a legend intended to remind aldermen to administer justice without favor or fear. His 'Arrest of the Corrupt Judge' was believed to have symbolic reference to the trial, torture and execution of Pieter Lanchals and other officials accused of engaging in corrupt activity in support of Maximilian. The careful attention to detail in his paintings is thought by some to bear witness to his affection for Bruges.

"Hans Memling lived and created great works of art in the city until his death in 1494, becoming rich as well as enormously popular.

"Bruges had become a world center of manuscript illumination, a place held until 1520. Illuminated books included histories, romances, chronicles, and translations of Aristotle, Xenophon, and Petrarch as well as religious works. Illuminated manuscripts produced in quantity for export gave employment to painters of miniature art as well as to bookbinders and calligraphers.

"Light Spanish wool imported to supplement dwindling English imports stimulated the ailing textile industry. When England transferred its wool staple to Bruges from Calais in 1558, the industry received another boost.

"In 1520, the Zwin silted up so completely it was no longer navigable. In the years that followed, the city commissioned a series of plans to reopen it or to construct a new canal. City magistrates hired Jan Provoost to make topographic drawings of Bruges and Marcus Gheeraerts to create a plan of the city, but no effective actions followed. The city treasury was too empty from the prolonged conflict with Maximilian to afford the enormous expense of dredging the Zwin or constructing a new canal to the sea.

"Antwerp was now the commercial hub for international trade. However, realistic Bruges merchants developed a cooperative relationship with the new commercial center and conducted their business in that city. With luxurious textiles no longer Bruges' main source of wealth, trade guilds having to do with foodstuffs and river navigation sprang up and prospered. Portugal, the Mediterranean, and the Baltic regions were now major focuses of business.

"That is not to suggest that Bruges returned to its earlier prosperity. True, there were wealthy families and wealthy merchants, but its diminished role in world trade severely hurt the city.

"By 1544, the population had shrunk to 30,000 and a quarter of those were living in poverty."

Sixteenth Century Artists

Return to the Dijver for another visit to the museums.

In the Gruuthuse Museum you will find the topographic drawings of Bruges by Jan Provost and Marcus Gheeraerts.

Magnificent paintings by Gerard David and Hieronymous Bosch are found in the Groeninge Museum. The collection of

Memling's works is in the Memling Museum of Saint John's Hospital on Mariastraat.

Foreign Merchants

Portuguese and English Nation Houses were located on Spinolarei near Spanjaardstraat.

To get there from Dijver: As you exit the Gruuthuse Museum walk to the main street. This will be Dijver. Turn right and continue straight ahead. The street name will change to Predikherenstraat. At Peerdenstraat turn left and cross the bridge. The Peerdenstraatbrug, built in 1294, is the oldest bridge in the city. Cross Hoogstraat and the street name changes to Ridderstraat. Further along, the street name becomes Engelese. Continue on Engelese to Spinolarei and turn left. Many foreign nation houses and private homes are in this area.

Scottish Consulate – Sint Maartensplein next to Saint Walburgha Church.

To get there: Retrace your steps on Spinolarei to Koningstraat, one block beyond Engelese. Turn right and continue for one block. Saint Walburgha's and the former Scottish Consulate will be on your left.

Anselm Adornes, wealthy scion of a Genoese (Italian) clan, was both merchant and Scottish consul. As a diplomat representing Charles the Bold, he was a master negotiator and politician. Adornes loved Scotland and spent as much time as possible in that country. Murdered in Scotland, his heart was returned to Bruges. Adornes built the Jerusalem Chapel and the almshouses next to the church in 1483. Loyal supporters of the Burgundian rulers, Adornes family members had been an integral part of Bruges society since the 14th century.

Saint Walburgha Church, built by the Jesuits in the 17th century, replaced the original that was destroyed during the Reformation. A magnificent baroque structure, it contains an exquisitely carved wooden pulpit, carved marble communion bench, and paintings by Suvee and Caravaggio.

Jerusalem Church. To get there: On exiting Saint Walburgha, turn right, then immediately right again on Hoornstraat, right at the canal, right on Verversdijk and left on Sint Annakerkstraat. Saint Anne's is also a later church and well worth a visit. Turn right at the end of the church onto Jeruzalem-kerkstraat. Continue to Balstraat. The Jerusalem Church is on the left and beyond it is the Lace Museum at #11 Balstraat. Be sure to visit the lace school across Balstraat from the church on Peperstraat. Demonstrations are given each afternoon except Sunday.

Return to Jeruzalemstraat and turn right. Continue to Carmersstraat. Turn left on Carmersstraat, (the Pas Partout Restaurant is on the corner), cross the Sint Annarei canal and pick up Genthof on the other side. It has been a long walk and you are probably ready for rest and refreshment. At the corner of Genthof and Sint Annarei, stop at the Terrastje, a tiny family-owned pub, for garlic mussels and Leffe Blond beer unless it is a Monday or Tuesday when the pub is closed.

Genthof will become Academiestraat. Continue on Academiestraat to Vlamingstraat. Cross Vlamingstraat to enter Grauwwerkerstraat. On Grauwwerkerstraat, note the original 13th century facade on #2. At #4, the Romanesque lower floor is also original, probably dating from around 1000. Number six was the home of the great Humanist Juan Luis Vives whom you will hear about in the next chapter.

Hof Bladelin. Like Anselm Adornes and Louis Gruuthuse, Pieter Bladelin was a wealthy merchant, politician, and diplomat. Municipal treasurer under Philip the Good, he also managed the duke's finances.

To get there: Continue along Grauwwerkerstraat to Naaldenstraat. Turn left at Naaldenstraat. Hof Bladelin is at #19. The mansion is now a home for the elderly. Ring the bell to the right of the door. An attendant will let you into the courtyard, one of the earliest examples of Renaissance architecture in Belgium.

Bladelin built the house in mid-1400 and sold it to the Italian banking family, the Medici's, around 1466. The Florentines converted the courtyard into an early Renaissance palazzo. Note the medallions of Lorenzo de Medici and his wife, Clarice Orsini.

If you look up as you leave you will see a tower on the palace. This was not built for prestige or decoration, but to serve as a lookout for ships coming into the city that might owe tolls or taxes to the owner of the house. Many of the great houses from the Middle Ages had similar towers.

To return to the Markt, turn right as you leave Hof Bladelin and continue on Naaldenstraat. At Sint Jakobsstraat, turn left and proceed straight ahead until you come to the Markt. Turn right and choose any of the fine restaurants on the square for your lunch or dinner or, for an unforgettable culinary experience, cross the Markt, enter Wollestraat and walk one half block to Oude Burg. Turn right. At #14, in a restored 16th century cellar, the 't Voermanshuus Restaurant serves gourmet Belgian cuisine that will leave your senses tingling. Keep in mind that most restaurants close at 2:30 p.m. and open again at 6:00 p.m.

Chapter Thirteen

"The gulf between rich and poor widened," I said.

"Yes. Under Count Philip I, the city, like a sick person, was recovering from its overwhelming losses. Healing had begun, but unfortunately, his reign lasted only twelve years.

"He married Joanna of Castile, and became sole heir to the kingdoms of Aragon and Castile in Spain, an ominous note for Bruges and for the country."

"Ominous?" I asked. "But why? How could his marriage hurt Bruges?"

"Be patient," said Anders, laughing at my eagerness. "You'll understand before I'm finished."

"Philip's six-year-old son, Charles V, succeeded his father on his death in 1506. In 1515, Charles was declared of age and presented to the Netherlands by his grandfather, Maximilian, at the latter's palace in Brussels. Hope rose in Bruges that the city would again have a sympathetic ruler who, like his father, would be dedicated and innovative.

"Within four years after presentation at court, two events occurred that would alter the destiny of Bruges and all of the Netherlands for centuries. Both of Charles' grandfathers, Maximilian I and Ferdinand of Aragon, died, leaving the youth an incredible inheritance. By 1519, Charles V ruled an empire that encompassed the imperial Germanic lands, the Netherlands, Burgundy, Spain, Naples, Sicily, and Spanish possessions in the New World.

"The Flemings still thought of Charles as their Burgundian prince and assumed Flanders would be his chief concern. Charles knew he must nurture the territory for it was the most highly developed, the wealthiest, and the most complex of all his possessions. He needed its resources to support the rest of his empire and the wars in which he was perpetually engaged to defend its borders.

"However, problems in other parts of the empire demanded so much of his attention he was compelled to travel constantly, visiting Flanders, the land of his birth, only five times between 1522 and 1555. He spent only 10 years total in Flanders during the 40 years of his reign and very little of that in Bruges. His aunt, Margaret of Austria, governed the region until her death at age 50.

"The people of Bruges loved Charles. In 1528, the Franc of Bruges paid tribute to their beloved monarch by commissioning a magnificent chimneypiece designed by Lancelot Blondeel. The wooden carving commemorated Flanders' release in 1529 from its feudal relationship with France, a triumph for Charles and for the country. The imposing sculpture still adorns the Aldermen's Room in the former Palace of the Liberty of Bruges on the Burg.

"Bruges did reasonably well under Charles. Prosperous Spanish merchant families who had resided in the city for centuries remained loyal throughout its difficult years. Local merchants established trading connections with several Spanish cities and light wool imported from Spain created employment for thousands. Demand for luxury products was high. Especially sought were the brilliantly illuminated manuscripts for which Bruges had become famous.

"Then an event occurred that shattered the unity of the Catholic Church and upset the equilibrium of Catholic Europe."

"Was that the Reformation?" I asked.

"That's right. In 1517, Martin Luther, a German monk deeply troubled by the corruption of the Roman Catholic Church, nailed 95 theses to a church door in Wittenberg attacking the sale of indulgences and other traditional practices of the Church. His act heralded the Reformation and the social upheaval that followed. Like many revolutionaries, Luther did not want to leave the Catholic Church; he wanted it freed from baseness and brought back to the simple teachings of Christ.

"His action reflected the temper of the times. The Church was losing its control over people. Dependence of followers on the Church's infallibility was being subtly eroded as people began to question what had formerly been accepted. The weakening could also be seen in small changes that, in the aggregate, were powerful. One homely example came with the invention of the clock. Ringing of bells to regulate peoples' activities, a responsibility held by the Church, was no longer needed. The invention of mechanical timepieces caused the omnipresence of the Church to recede ever so slightly.

"Luther's teachings, brought to Flanders by German traders and soldiers and followed by those of John Calvin, spread in the region like flood from a North Sea storm. Calvin's position was even more uncompromising than Rome's. An austere man, he was convinced that complete restructuring of church and society were the only solutions for the decadence of the medieval Church. Certain the Church would be strengthened by discipline, he advocated avoidance of worldly pleasures – there would be no singing, no dancing, no drinking."

"That must have been quite a departure for the beer drinking Flemings," I said.

Anders nodded and chuckled, then became serious again.

"It would seem so, but he gained an impressive following. Charles V, however, would have none of it. He adamantly condemned the new movement as heretical and assumed the posture of staunch defender of the Catholic faith. He issued edicts ordering death for anyone other than clergy who even discussed theology or failed to denounce heretics.

"In 1527 Bruges' first Protestant martyr was burned at the stake on the Burg. Yet, despite the threat of capital punishment, the new religion continued to spread.

"Even as he ordered punishments, Charles knew that ruthless persecution would force his most intelligent and creative citizens to emigrate. Consequently, he was lenient about enforcing his pronouncements, unlike his son and successor, Philip II. Nobility and foreign merchants were entirely exempt from his rulings."

The old historian sighed, closed his eyes, then opened them, and continued.

"In spite of the tension and uncertainty brought on by the Reformation, master painters Hugo Van der Goes, Jan Provoost and Marcus Geeraerts continued to live and work in the city. However, Bruges lost two of its most illustrious painters in the early sixteenth century. The great artist Gerard David died in 1523 and Jan Provost in 1529."

He was silent for several seconds.

"Didn't Humanism become important about this time?" I asked.

"Yes," he said, animated once more. "The movement flourished in the early 16th century as scholars rediscovered and reinterpreted the achievements of ancient Rome and Greece. It captured the imagination of a core of intellectuals in Bruges. For example, Anselm Adornes, the Scottish consul and wealthy international trader, copied Humanist manuscripts and read Humanist writings. Adornes was from an Italian family integrated into Bruges society since the 14th century. Mark Laurin, the central figure among a network of great intellects in Bruges was host to such illustrious scholars as Erasmus, Juan Luis Vives, and Thomas More. Joris Cassander, one of the first Humanist teachers, was also a visitor to Bruges.

"What made the movement so attractive?" I asked.

"Unlike the Catholic Church, Humanism was grounded in the belief that human beings are capable and essentially good. The Humanists were exceptional thinkers.

"These outstanding men brought practical ideas, as well. In the areas of education and care of the poor their thoughts led to the establishment of schools for children of less affluent families and to the creation of centers for the study of Greek, Latin and Hebrew. Juan Luis Vives defended the right of women to have a university education and introduced the revolutionary idea that girls of noble families were intelligent as boys.

"Vives was a Spanish Jew born in 1492 who emigrated from Spain when Jews were ordered to become Christian or leave the country. Despite his parents' conversion to Christianity, fanatic Spanish inquisitors burned his father alive. While studying at the Sorbonne in Paris, Juan Luis learned of the Spanish community in Bruges from one of his professors and made the city his home.

"The Protestant break with Catholicism engendered enormous interest and frequent discussion within the Humanist circle. Because of their influence, city officials in Bruges were more enlightened than in many parts of the country. Freedom of thought and discussion were permitted to continue and King Charles did not interfere with the city's liberal policies. Charles' edicts were not ignored, but city officials were pragmatists. They knew that businessmen and foreign traders who had returned to the city would not tolerate a rigid, repressive policy."

"This must have been a challenging time for Bruges' leaders," I said.

"Of course." he replied. "Even more for the people. For those who did not take up the new religion, little changed. For those who did, everything changed. Practicing Protestantism could mean death. Between 1517 and 1572, 70 Anabaptists from the poorest parts of Bruges were executed.

"By 1555, Charles was weary and racked with gout. He abdicated his title of ruler of the Holy Roman Empire and turned over the governments of the Netherlands, Spain, Italy, and the Indies to his Spanish-born son, Philip II, in a lavish ceremony held in Brussels. The Netherlands at that time was strong, rich, and at peace.

"Supported on the arm of William of Orange, later to become the arch-enemy of his dynasty, Charles presented Philip at court as the new ruler of the Netherlands. Brugeans would look back on this occasion with deep sadness. Under Philip's rule, they would lose their freedom, their autonomy, and their finest minds.

"Charles retired to a remote monastery in the wooded hills north of the Tagus Valley in Spain to spend his final years in quiet and meditation. He had been the most prominent king in Europe for 40 years, yet could not establish unity and order in his extensive realm. In his prime, he had ruled domains that stretched from Vienna to the Atlantic in a patchwork of governmental units having different customs and degrees of political autonomy. He died in 1558 of a fever."

Tribute to Charles V

On the Burg, enter the Archives (Stadsarchief) located in the Palace of the Liberty of Bruges near the Visitors' Center. The Liberty of Bruges and the Franc of Bruges are synonymous. Liberty of Bruges is the English translation of Brugse Vrije. Franc de Bruges is the French translation. Signs inside the

Archives will direct you to the Renaissance (Alderman's) Room where you will find a chimneypiece sculpted in wood, marble, and alabaster designed by Lancelot Blondeel.

The Brugse Vrije (Liberty of Bruges) commissioned the piece as a tribute to the beloved ruler, Charles V, probably in appreciation for his part in freeing Flanders from its feudal relationship with France.

A life size statue of Charles, carved of wood, dominates the piece. His paternal grandparents, Maximilian of Austria and Mary of Burgundy, and his maternal grandparents, Isabella of Castile and Ferdinand of Aragon, stand on either side. Many other figures and medallions adorn this superb work of art.

Marc Laurin's Palace

Exit the Burg on Breidelstraat. Turn left at Wollestraat and right on Oude Burg. Number 27 was built by Jan III de Baenst in the mid-15th century and owned by Marc Laurin, Lord of Watervliet in the 16th century. The palace is now a hotel.

The Spanish Presence

Spanjaardstraat, as the name suggests, was an enclave of the Spaniards. The Hotel Navarra was the home of Juan de Peralta. Hof de la Torre at #16, the Castilian Nation House was purchased in 1494 by the city for the Castilians; De Pijnappel at #9 Spanjaardstraat was the home of Gonzalo de Aguilan.

To get there from Oude Burg: Looking toward the Markt, take Oude Burg to Wollestraat, turn left on Wollestraat, cross the Markt to Vlamingstraat, turn right on Academiestraat and left on Spanjaardstraat. If you have reached Jan van Eyckplein, you have gone too far.

Chapter Fourteen

"Charles V was a great ruler, yet you say that under his son, the people of Bruges would lose all that was most important to them. How could this be? Would not the son have learned the right way to govern from his talented father?"

"I suspect his father taught him little. Remember that Charles was away most of the time, tending the empire, while Philip II remained in Spain, being brought up by Spaniards.

"Philip looked Flemish, but he was Spanish through and through and spoke neither French nor Dutch. At his inauguration in Brussels in 1555, he had to respond through interpreters. He was awkward and shy, repelling love rather than attracting it as his father had done.

"On his inaugural visit to Bruges, he stood in front of the Market Hall on a stage that had been decorated by the celebrated painter Peter Pourbus. Interpreters recounted his solemn oath to maintain the city's rights and privileges. It was an empty promise.

"Philip had been raised in the tradition of centrally executed power. Spain was an absolutist monarchy and he was groomed to be a centralist ruler. He had no special affection for his subjects in the Netherlands nor did he understand them. Their love of freedom and independence and the democratic traditions of the cities were foreign to him.

"A fanatical defender of the Catholic faith, he vowed to stamp out heresy and destroy Protestantism. He tolerated no leniency, but demanded ruthless enforcement of his father's edicts and added more of his own. He neither understood nor cared that his cruelty would force out the brightest and best of his Flemish people. His goal was to protect the unity of the Catholic Church at any cost.

"He regarded Flemings as an obstinate and uncooperative race. Instead of valuing their talents and wealth as assets that could strengthen his empire as his father had done, he was determined to control them. He vowed to break the people by any means whatever although it might destroy their economy and deprive him of an important source of income.

"By 1564, the situation had reached crisis proportions. William of Orange, leader of the Protestants, searched for allies to mount a revolt against Spain.

"Despite Philip's orders that his edicts be even more cruelly applied, Catholics turned to the new religion by the thousands, pursuing their new faith in secret.

"On April 5, 1566, a body of armed men approached the residence of Margaret of Parma, regent of the Netherlands after Margaret of Austria, and presented to her a manifesto demanding an end to the inquisition. Frightened, she agreed to reduce the severity of punishments for heresy and to write Philip in Spain asking for relief from his edicts.

"Protestants practicing underground in the Netherlands took this as a signal to come out in astounding numbers. Fiery preachers aroused followers to a crazed fury, urging them to destroy anything they believed idolatrous. Throughout Flanders, Protestants shattered images, decapitated statues, smashed stained glass windows, demolished altar screens, and shredded vestments in violent demonstrations of their rage. The havoc they wreaked trying to force their own places of worship continued for a month.

"At the height of the destruction, a handful of Bruges burghers armed themselves and closed the city gates. Bruges escaped most of the pillage and its important treasures remained intact.

"Count Egmont, an appointee of Margaret of Parma, responded to the Protestant iconoclasts in the rest of Flanders by destroying Protestant churches and hanging Calvinists."

"Nevertheless, by 1566, Calvinists had established a foothold in Bruges. The Humanist influence among the city's most powerful administrative officers gave the city more tolerant policies than other communities. The combined power of these policies and the determination of the city council overrode the narrow power base of the dissidents. Wholesale destruction that ravaged other cities did not occur in Bruges and Protestants were left alone as long as they neither worshipped publicly nor damaged church property. Freedom of religion was practiced in the city until 1578.

"In the meantime, Philip in Spain brooded over the situation in the Netherlands, angry with its people's independent stance and Protestant leanings. Determined to teach them a lesson they would never forget, he sent the Duke of Alva into the Low Countries in 1567 with a mandate to tame his intractable subjects at any cost. He ordered Alva to destroy urban privileges, substitute royal for urban officials, disband local militias, and raise taxes.

"The duke, a cold, cruel, proud man intent on laying waste to the country, entered the South with 9000 troops as if invading a hostile, occupied territory rather than a country whose citizens were loyal to their king.

"Alva set up a 'Blood Council,' a committee of nine members controlled by three Spaniards, over which he presided. The Council, whose purpose was to arrest and punish rebels and suppress disorder, ignored the traditions, privileges, and rights of the people. In an unprecedented bloodbath between 1567 and 1569, he executed nearly 6000 Netherlanders.

"Alva's reign of terror forced many of the most energetic, talented Protestants to flee the South for the northern provinces where natural defenses of the land prevented his troops from reaching them. The provinces of Zeeland and Holland were actually groups of islands surrounded by land reclaimed from the sea. At will, rebels could open sluice gates in the dikes and flood the lowlands forcing the Spanish army to flee or drown.

"In Bruges, foreign merchants were not damaged by the Duke of Alva's terrorism, but they were disgusted with the blatant interference of Spanish churchmen in civic affairs. They finally left for ports that were more favorable. However, Bruges had not yet lost its most brilliant citizens.

"Brugeans had great affection for the Spanish traders and scholars who had been an integral part of the community for centuries. However, Alva's cruelty and high-handedness produced powerful anti-Spanish sentiment even among the conservative Catholics in Bruges. The duke ignored the city's traditional privileges, instituted onerous financial reforms, and garrisoned Spanish soldiers in the city. Tension increased like a tightly drawn rubber band.

"Yet repeated efforts at resistance failed, even when mounted in cooperation with Ghent and Ypres .

"On the other hand, Spain was not able to prevail against the northern provinces. Overrun by fanatical Calvinists, the North successfully defied Alva with well-organized, disciplined leaders who created their own government and gradually restored order and trade. The South, with no natural defenses and failed opposition, remained subject to the Spanish crown.

"In 1576, leaders launched an effort to join the North and South in a united front to expel the Spaniards, but the Catholic South and the Protestant North could not reach agreement. Traditions of regional autonomy added to the impasse, once more preventing a united Netherlands from protecting itself. The northern provinces saw themselves as a separate entity and refused to aid their southern cousins.

"Nevertheless, rebellion against Spain continued in the southern cities. The number of Protestants mushroomed and Protestantism became a force of growing power.

"Calvinist radicals took over Ghent in 1577. In March of 1578, troops from Ghent entered Bruges, replacing the city council and organizing a revolutionary committee.

Now able to espouse their religion openly, Calvinist persecution of Catholics in the city nearly matched Spain's persecution of Protestants. Franciscan monks were imprisoned, tortured, and burned at the stake; three were whipped and forced out of the city; nine were banished. When protests arose, priests, monks and friars were ordered to leave and given three days to gather their belongings. Only a few of the smaller monastic communities were allowed to remain. Calvinists demolished the Franciscan monastery and forbade the exercise of Catholicism. The ancient religion nearly died during the six years of Protestant domination.

"Protestants closed or demolished several small chapels. They sacked Saint Walburgha's Church and destroyed Saint Anne's although both were rebuilt in later years. They closed the Chapel of the Holy Blood, used the crypt as a prison, and turned the Church of Our Lady into a stable for soldier's horses.

"Saint Basil's was robbed of gold and silver and the shrine that held the relic of the holy blood, made of gold and imbedded with precious stones, was taken. Juan Perez de Malvenda, a resident of Bruges, secreted the precious relic of the holy blood in his home until the storm of religious fanaticism passed.

"Still Philip would not release his hold on the Netherlands. In 1579, he appointed Alexander Farnese as governor of his problem territory. A brilliant military commander, Farnese subdued the southern cities, one by one, using siege instead of bloodshed as his weapon.

"By 1580, all foreign merchants had left Bruges for Antwerp, artisans were gone in great numbers, the weary people were decimated by plague, their commerce was destroyed and the population had shrunk to 29,000.

"In 1584, Bruges submitted to Farnese. Once more under the yoke of Catholic Spain, the consequences were catastrophic. The last of its most brilliant citizens, fearing a repeat of Spanish brutality, fled to the United Provinces, a loss that culturally impoverished the city and added one more link to its chain of decline. The emigration of the brilliant mathematician and scientist, Simon Stevin, was a tragic loss for the city. He conducted pioneering research in countless disciplines including bookkeeping, navigation, astronomy, engineering, and development of the decimal system. Had he remained, his creative genius might have helped the city recover.

"The loss of its best minds and separation from the northern provinces plummeted Bruges into the rank of a poor provincial town. Thousands lived in misery and went hungry despite the presence of wealthy monastic orders and a core of historically rich families.

"During the 158 year reign of the Spanish Habsburgs, around 80,000 inhabitants of the southern provinces emigrated. Many relocated to Germany and England, many more to Holland.

"To improve defenses against Protestant fanatics, city magistrates in Bruges ordered all buildings demolished outside the town walls within a specified distance. Many religious institutions in the affected areas sought and received shelter and security inside the city. Cistercians, Carmelites, Capuchins, and Jesuits all came in this period and some of the more affluent orders brought precious artifacts and other wealth with them.

"The savage cruelty and ruthless repression of the Duke of Alva disappeared when he was recalled, but the interests, views and wishes of the Flemish people continued to be ignored by their Spanish rulers. Philip's fanatical posture allowed little concern for economic well being and banned freedom of speech that might introduce controversial ideas. The permeation of art, literature, drama and architecture by religion stifled creativity although religious art that met the church's prescriptions flourished."

The old historian became quiet. His eyes took on a sad, almost mournful quality.

After several moments, I said, "This must have been a terribly discouraging time for the people of Bruges."

"Yes," he answered. "For all the Southern Netherlands, unless you were Catholic and followed the rules carefully. Survival became the central issue. Development of the mind was possible only along a single track. The Church's."

The Market Hall

On the Markt, the Market Hall spreads out from the base of the belfry as if it were a part of the tower. Standing on a platform in front of the Market Hall, Philip II made promises he could not or would not keep.

Home of Juan Perez de Malvenda

The precious relic of the Holy Blood was secreted in de Malvenda's home at 53 Wollestraat during the Protestant uprising. Enter Wollestraat from the Markt. His home was the last building on the left.

Chapter Fourteen

Simon Stevin

A statue and square are devoted to this remarkable genius. To get there from the Markt: Enter Steenstraat and walk two blocks. Simon Stevinplein is on the left. Several excellent restaurants on the square make this a good place to rest and refresh.

Chapter Fifteen

"When was the Southern Netherlands formally separated from the North?" I asked.

"The Truce of 1609 recognized the northern Netherlands as a separate entity, the United Provinces. Then, in 1648 the Treaty of Munster between Spain and the United Provinces confirmed its independence. The treaty officially separated the South from its cousins in the North.

"England and the United Provinces had formed an alliance to contain the expansionist ambitions of the French kings and looked on the Southern Netherlands as a buffer between their countries and France. The consequences for the South were terrible. Its soil became a battleground in all but 29 years of the period between 1566 and 1713.

"Bruges opened negotiations with England, the Hanseatic towns, and the Dutch in an attempt to restore trading relations, but the efforts were unsuccessful. All thought Bruges too likely to be attacked by France.

"By 1620, emigration, disease and war had reduced the population of Bruges to 27,000. Warring armies had ravaged the countryside around the town although defensive structures that encircled the city saved it from similar destruction. Bastions provided inner defenses and a combination of bastions and ravelins interspersed with stone structures deterred invasion. Access to the city was only through its medieval gates.

"The Dutch – the new United Provinces – resoundingly defeated Spain in 1639 in a battle at sea and took possession of the left bank of the river Scheldt, cutting off Bruges from its main connection to the North Sea. When the medieval foreport of Sluis was lost as well, the city's access to the sea was completely shut down.

"This would seem the death blow for the city, but entrepreneurial Bruges merchants once more found ways to survive. They turned to opportunities that opened with Spain's occupation of Flanders. Trading companies created branches in Lisbon, Cadiz, Seville, and other cities and gained access to trade with the New World. Some Bruges merchants made fabulous fortunes, even enabling them to become Spanish aristocrats.

"Later, while still under Spanish rule, a network of canals was built that once more linked Bruges and other cities to the North Sea and to the countryside between the coast and the cities. A new town dock built in 1664 facilitated trading and Bruges' modest maritime recovery began.

"Little new construction but a great deal of restoration and conversion occurred in the 17th century. Stone or brick gradually replaced wooden houses and fire-prone thatched roofs give way to tile. Wooden dwellings at the beguinage were converted to brick and stone cottages.

"In the 18th century several elegant townhouses were built and wooden frontages continued to be replaced with brick facades. The town began to take on a baroque and classical appearance. However, lack of funds left many medieval palaces to decay. A few would be restored late in the century."

"It sounds as though the city was beginning to recover," I said. "Did it continue?"

"Not in a straight line and not permanently. It would begin, then stop, depending on who was in power. For a hundred years, the Southern Netherlands was like a bouncing ball, first under the rule of one country, then under another.

"The series of wars ended in 1713. Six years later, the Treaty of Utrecht assigned the territory to the Austrian Emperor, Charles VI, a descendant of Charles V.

"France still coveted the South. In 1744 her troops entered the Southern Netherlands and occupied it until 1748. Under French rule, Bruges became a mausoleum. Trade and shipping were cut off and two thirds of the people were living in poverty. The French doubled taxes, imposed new ones, and conscripted the city's men into the army.

"Fortunately, the French turned over the South to Austria in 1748.

"The Austrian ruler of Flanders, Charles of Lorraine, gained great favor with the people of Bruges by improving canals and establishing a herring fishery, but the town's wealthy citizens, who had become inordinately conservative, did nothing to help the city. They hoarded their wealth, unwilling even to risk it in trading ventures. Adding to the town's woes, Holland suppressed Bruges' recovery by stubbornly keeping the Scheldt River closed.

"Joseph II of Austria, who followed Charles of Lorraine, was a sensible and liberal ruler. He improved roads, instituted measures that prohibited the exclusivism of the guilds and attempted to stimulate trade, although his efforts were unsuccessful. Unfortunately, he imposed his changes from above without preparation of the people. When he tried to do away with the old regional government and the sacred privileges for which so much blood had been shed, the people balked. For the first time in over 100 years, the Estates General met in an abortive attempt to declare the Southern Netherlands an independent state. Sadly, they could not agree among themselves, nor had they any experience in self-government.

Anders paused, then sighed deeply before continuing.

"Although reconquered by the Austrians at the end of 1790, France again gained possession of the territory in 1794. In 1795, the Southern Netherlands became part of the revolutionary French Republic.

"For 20 years France swallowed up Flanders. French revolutionaries put in place an autocratic system of governance that suffocated the spirit of Bruges as brutally as the Spanish had done. In all fairness, however, they did make some changes that improved society.

"The French removed historical divisions of the country, eliminated counties and duchies and replaced the old regional divisions with nine *départements* that would later become Belgian provinces. They threw out privileges of the nobility, did away with guilds and their monopolies, and dispensed with torture as a means of enforcing the law.

"Most of the power of the Catholic Church was abolished. Tragically, ancient Saint Donatian's church was taken down brick by brick as a symbol of the *Ancien Régime*, an iconoclastic act that took years to complete. Revolutionaries destroyed the statues painted by Van Eyck that had adorned the niches of the Town Hall from the 14th century.

"The State confiscated and sold church property making it available for development and creating a huge change in land ownership. The beneficiaries were not the peasants and the poor, however, but the nobility and bourgeoisie who made fortunes from the redistribution of land.

"The French closed churches, persecuted priests, silenced bells and eliminated Sunday Schools. Monastic orders ceased to exist except for a few that staffed hospitals. "Reason" instead of religion was worshipped, but efforts to force clergy to swear hatred of the monarchy failed.

"Anyone who wanted to progress in the new regime had to speak French. The language was taught in schools in keeping with Napoleon's idea of developing a strong pro-French ruling class. The French suppressed the growth of a Dutch-speaking middle class and encouraged a middle class tied to French ideas and French culture."

"But I see signs in Dutch on all the streets. Publications are in Dutch. It seems to be the language of choice today," I said.

"That's right. In the 19th century, the priest and poet Guido Gezelle wrote his extensive works in Dutch, causing renewed attention to be given the native language. Since 1885, Dutch has been the primary language of northern Belgium. Changing street names occurred only in the 20th century.

"Between 1792 and 1800, revolutionaries ransacked Flanders, taking treasures that ended in French museums. Military and tax burdens grew heavy and hostility toward the French heightened.

"By 1813 Napoleon's war with Austria and Russia was going badly. In 1814, Russians and Prussians entered the Low Countries and the French evacuated. Napoleon, defeated at Waterloo in 1815, left 45,000 dead and wounded on Netherlands soil. His capitulation ended the period of French domination."

Take a walk around the Markt, along Steenstraat and among residential areas. How many facades are dated in the 16th, 17th, or 18th centuries? Note the niches on the corners of buildings and the icons placed in them that, together with the numerous churches, gave the city an intensely Catholic ambience.

Return to the Burg. Revisit the remains of Saint Donatian's Cathedral in the Holiday Inn Crown Plaza Hotel. Observe the outline of the old church in the park. Look again at the model of the original edifice. Imagine the rage of the French revolutionaries, so determined to destroy symbols of the Ancien Régime (the old rule) they demolished a priceless piece of Bruges' history.

Chapter Sixteen

"When did the Southern Netherlands become an independent country?" I asked.

The old scholar stood and stretched. Then he eased into his chair again.

"Belgium was born in 1830. After Napoleon's defeat, the Congress of Vienna, comprised of the victors of the war, were adamant that the Northern and Southern Netherlands should be united under the Protestant ruler, William I of Orange. They argued that it was necessary in order to form a barrier against France, an exceedingly unpopular decision, especially in Catholic Bruges. After 200 years of separation, the notion of being ruled by a Dutch king who was also a Protestant, engendered support only from the town's small Protestant community.

"Nevertheless, the plan was followed and William of Orange governed for 15 years. Opposition to Dutch rule climaxed in August of 1830 with a rebellion in Brussels. Dutch forces that should have put down the revolt had no enthusiasm for the task and in October quietly withdrew. Suddenly, for the first time in its turbulent 1800-year history, the Southern Netherlands was a fully independent state.

"When word of independence arrived in Bruges, the town rose from its apathy for a few brief hours. Rioting, pillaging, and joy raced through the town in equal measure.

Ecstatic citizens hoisted Belgium's flag of freedom on the belfry to proclaim its independence .

Unfortunately, the celebration was only a fleeting respite. Of the 43,000 people living in Bruges, fifteen thousand were on relief.

"The First Industrial Revolution between 1790 and 1850 was well under way and, in Belgium, productivity had leapt forward at an astounding rate – except in Bruges. Ghent and Antwerp industrialized and grew stronger. Bruges, clinging to its home-based industries, fell asleep and missed the industrial revolution entirely.

"Traditional cottage industries, the centuries-old backbone of textile production, were like ants competing with elephants. Although textile producers had, over the years, broadened their products to include linen and cotton as well as wool, the home-based enterprises were hopeless against the mammoth output of new English factories.

"When bank failure aborted the town's most ambitious industrializing effort, the city's entrepreneurs, hurt too many times in the past, became even more cautious and invested in trading ventures rather than modern industry.

"Around the same time, conservative Catholics won every seat on the city council, replacing the more forward looking Protestants.

"By the middle of the 19th century, it seemed nothing more could happen. Business had been beaten down and relief rolls had ballooned. Then the linen market failed, striking the final blow. The industry was thrust into chaos with thousands of flax-spinners and weavers working for starvation wages. Linen export in Flanders between 1846 and 1896 dropped by half. The work force in flax diminished from 60,000 to 22,900.

"Misery and suffering scarred the town from 1845 to 1850. Ten thousand lacemakers, unable to find other employment, toiled 12 hours a day and were paid too little to buy enough food to keep from starving. Many resorted to prostitution in order to feed their families. In 1847, gangs of starving residents plundered bakeries and granaries.

"As if economic depression was not enough, potato disease destroyed the chief food of the poor. Outbreaks of cholera and typhoid were daily occurrences. Flight from the countryside into Bruges swelled its population to 50,000 by 1850 with 40 per cent of the population on poor relief. Refugees found temporary housing in wooden barracks on the Markt and the Zand.

"Once the wealthiest city of Flanders, Bruges was now the poorest."

The fire crackled and a yellow flame spread along the log. As I stared into the fireplace, I could almost see the desperation of the people.

"How did the city recover from such disasters?" I asked.

He was silent.

"It should have decayed and disappeared," I continued, "but it's gorgeous, like a museum. Full of animated, intelligent people who seem to be economically comfortable."

"When men and women get beaten down," he said, "they often become blind to the good things in their midst. Sometimes it takes outsiders to open their eyes.

"English travelers in the mid-19th century, attracted by the community's cultural history, discovered streets lined with decaying, ancient buildings that had not been victimized by the plaster and paint and ugly refurbishing that had swept through other medieval cities. A wave of modernization that lessened the beauty of many European medieval towns missed Bruges entirely.

"After decades of poverty and suffering, few townspeople paid attention to the cultural treasures surrounding them or recognized their value. Where they saw decaying buildings ripe for demolition, the English recognized reminders of greatness that should be preserved.

"Real estate prices were rock bottom and servants could be retained for 25 per cent less than in England. English military and colonial retirees, finding they could live far better in Bruges on their government pensions than in Britain, began a stream of immigration.

"By 1869, the English colony had grown to 1200 and boasted its own tearooms, schools, chapels, theater, seminary, and cemetery.

"Hadn't there always been a relationship between Bruges and England?" I asked.

"Historically, of course. English interest in Bruges started long ago, probably beginning with its ancient trading relationship with the city. As you know, English wool was essential for producing the fine woolen textiles for which the town was famous in the Middle Ages.

"The city also had important English visitors. In the 15th century, Louis Gruuthuse entertained King Edward IV of England. From 1656 to 1659, Charles II, exiled king of England, found refuge in the city. In 1662, English nuns of the Order of Saint Francis settled in Bruges to escape the persecution of Oliver Cromwell's forces. The Prinsenhof, former residence of the Dukes of Burgundy, became their convent.

"The affluent, educated immigrants of the 19th century were steeped in a tradition of appreciation for art and history and worked vigorously to preserve the ancient structures and artifacts. They awakened the townspeople to the city's medieval beauty and captured their imagination.

"James Weale, a tireless, irascible English scholar and art lover, led in the study of the city's artistic heritage. In 1862, he authored the seminal work, *"Bruges et ses Environs,"* that drew broad attention to the value of its ancient buildings. John Steinmetz, another English immigrant, acquired an impressive collection of paintings and drawings;

Robert Chantrell created plans in neo-Roman style for the fire-damaged tower of Saint Savior's Church.

"Weale and a group of friends became founders of the *Société Archéologique*, an association dedicated to acquiring a collection of ancient artifacts. In 1874, the city purchased the Gruuthuse mansion to house the collection. The Society's activism in staging exhibitions and artistic events had brought Bruges to the attention of Europe by the beginning of the 20th century.

"Academically oriented leadership with its interest in the town's brilliant past was fortunate for Bruges. It ignited a movement in the 1900s for research-based restoration that resulted in authentically restored historic buildings.

"In 1892, a small book by Georges Rodenbach of Paris added to Bruges' world visibility. A work of symbolism popular in the period, "*Bruges la Morte*" (Bruges the Dead), portrayed Bruges as a city that had died and become a shrine. A best seller, the book drew world travelers to the city in astonishing numbers.

"Tourism became an industry with the potential for pulling the city out of its mire. At the same time, politicians and intellectuals, mindful of the city's medieval affluence, argued that only a viable seaport would return the town to prosperity.

The conservative Catholic council that came to power in 1876 successfully campaigned for a new seaport at Brugge-Zeehaven. Parliament approved their proposal and building begun in 1896 was completed in 1904. The plan included a canal that linked Zeebrugge with the docks in Bruges.

"Fortunately, the council did not discount the role of tourism. They were as committed to returning Bruges to its historic beauty as to building the new harbor. Conservation and restoration of historical buildings received a powerful stimulus.

"Some new construction in neo-gothic style was also done during this period, reflecting the influence of Europe's gothic revival. The Minnewater Clinic, the Provincial Court on the Markt, the State Teacher Training College and the upper level of the Chapel of the Holy Blood were all designed in neo-gothic style.

"Restoration and conservation efforts followed no planned agenda through most of the 20th century and some historical buildings were lost. Even in the 1960s, ancient buildings that had become derelict and abandoned blemished the City Center. Finally, in the 1970's, Bruges gave buildings of historical importance protective status and in 1971 established a Municipal Conservation and Restoration Department. Cobblestone streets replaced asphalt, statues filled the empty niches of the Town Hall, and tourists received assistance in the rebuilt Palace of the Liberty of Bruges.

"Little architectural decay remains now. Matching grants for home improvement and vacancy taxes motivate citizens to maintain their properties."

"How did the two world wars affect the city?" I asked.

"In 1914, German forces invaded the city and occupied it until compelled to retreat in 1918. The British, as part of an offensive strategy, bombed the harbor at Zeebrugge during the German occupation. The Germans again occupied Bruges during World War II and blew up the rebuilt harbor prior to retreat.

"Allied forces avoided bombing parts of cities that had historical significance, thus sparing Bruges' Center City. The Germans also left the Center City relatively untouched except for the looting of ancient artifacts. They stole Michelangelo's statue of the Virgin and Child and several masterpieces from Our Lady's Church. All were found and returned soon after the end of World War II. The Virgin and Child, discovered in an Austrian salt mine in 1945, found its way back to the city undamaged."

"What was the fate of Zeebrugge?" I asked.

"Zeebrugge was rebuilt still again in 1944, but by the 1960's it was outdated. Between 1972 and 1984 an entirely new, modern and enlarged harbor was created at a cost of more than 2 billion dollars. By the year 2000, activity in the harbor had increased to such an extent, Antwerp complained that Zeebrugge (and thus Bruges) was taking away her trade. Ironic, isn't it?" He slowly shook his head. "History repeating itself."

* * * * *

"That brings you to the present," he said. "I'm tired now and should retire. Yes, Miriam, I'll be along in a minute. Just another sip of wine."

The old scholar's eyes twinkled with merriment in spite of his fatigue.

"There's nothing like a good glass of wine. Good for the arteries. Pour me another glass, will you?" He delicately sniffed its soft aroma.

"Ah, bliss." Moments later, his eyelids drooped. I gently removed the glass from his withered hand and set it on the table beside his chair, then silently turned off my tape recorder, slipped it into its case and tiptoed to the door. Miriam was waiting.

"Thank you," she said. Our eyes met, we smiled, and I walked into the crisp, starry Belgian night.

Bruges la Morte

The house chosen by Rodenbach as the residence for his protagonist, Hugues Viane, in the novel, "Bruges la Morte," is located on Jan van Eyckplein.

To get there: From the Markt, take Vlamingstraat to Academiestraat. Turn right on Academiestraat. Go straight ahead for two blocks and you will be on Jan van Eyckplein. The statue of Van Eyck will be facing you. Behind the statue and slightly to the left is the fictitious home of the fictitious Hugues Viane. A reddish building, it is on the "V" of Kortewinkel and Spiegelrei.

Guido Gezelle Museum

To get there from Jan van Eyckplein: Take Spinolarei to Sint Annarei. Turn right, then left on Strostraat. Follow Strostraat to Jeruzalemstraat. Turn right on Jeruzalemstraat and watch for Rolweg on the left. Turn left onto Rolweg and continue straight ahead to #64 Rolweg. This will be several blocks.

You are near the Grand Canal that circles the Center City. There is an excellent path on the green belt that follows the canal. This may be a good time for a stroll or bicycle ride around the perimeter of the city or to the next main street if fatigue is setting in. The four remaining stilt windmills from the Middle Ages dominate the short section between the Kruispoort Gate (to the right along the green belt from the museum) and Dampoort (to the left along the green belt from the museum)

Lace

Bruges has been famous for its bobbin lace since the 16th century. If you did not get to the lace school and lace museum described at the end of Chapter 14, this would be a good time to visit them. Projects under way in the lace school will give you an appreciation of the skill, patience and work required to produce a lace collar or lace shawl. Demonstrations are given every afternoon except Sunday. The Arents Museum at ***#16*** *Dijver also has a fine selection of lace articles.*

Epilogue

The City Center gives one the feeling of time suspended. That Bruges has survived its violent past and two world wars with so much of its history preserved is nothing less than a miracle.

The city's exceptional beauty inspires the most callous visitor to wax poetic. Russet to ochre brick houses contrast with green trees, verdant lawns, and dark gray cobblestones. On clear, calm days the blue sky turns the network of canals into azure reflecting pools, doubling the visual pleasure of walls, bridges and water united in a richness of form and color. The medieval belfry on the Markt, rising 280 feet above the old Market Hall, makes an imposing focus of interest and the narrow streets that feed into it form an impressive contrast to the fine proportions of the square.

More than 3 million people tread the town's cobblestone streets each year, watch its medieval festivals, and learn a little of its noble history, yet the future of Bruges is still a question.

Will the success of the Zeebrugge harbor return the city to its historic prosperity? Most people think not, but on the other hand, neither can the future be predicted with any certainty. History has shown that unanticipated changes are fully capable of altering the course of a people in dramatic ways.

The 21st century is a time of vastly different political structures with differing values and expectations from those of the Middle Ages. Still, the rapid growth of trade brought by the harbor is giving a needed boost to the town's economy. Attracting modern companies that will establish themselves in the city and bring employment opportunities can be a powerful stimulus to the town's prosperity. To promote change without damaging the medieval ambience will be the challenge.

The citizens of Bruges are sometimes accused of having retained a small town mentality. If this is true, I am glad they have. I am glad they did not embrace the wave of modernization that would have transformed this jewel of the past into a bustling industrial metropolis like Brussels or Antwerp.

The people's suffering and misery were a terrible tragedy, yet their former poverty has permitted a glimpse into the character of a once astonishingly brilliant and wealthy medieval city. Its history of extravagant drama makes best-selling fiction pale by comparison.

Secret Corners of Bruges

Brochures from the Visitor's Bureau and travel guides from home will outline conventional walks to the most popular sites. This section will take you to places that tourists on short visits rarely reach. Historic places are italicized. There will be some overlap with directions to historic sites in the text.

Start at the *Smedenpoort Gate*. This medieval gate was built in 1295 and reconstructed in 1360. Note the skull attached to the left side of the passage. During a war with France in 1670, a traitor who tried to open the gate for the French army was beheaded and his skull mounted on the gate. An inner and an outer gate originally protected the city. Today only one remains, the outer wall destroyed in the 19th century.

Note the small building on the bank of the canal. Water borne diseases such as cholera devastated medieval towns. To improve the people's health, fresh water piped into the city from lakes in the countryside provided clean drinking water, a major innovation. Water was pumped by means of twenty-five windmills stationed along the banks of the canal. Four survive. The building before you held a *pump and storage facility*.

Turn and proceed toward the Center City via *Smedenstraat*. Note the building at *#69*. If you look above the door you will see the date of construction, 1633, the period of Spanish occupation. As you continue on the street, note the religious icons placed in niches above the first floor of several buildings, a popular practice in Catholic Bruges.

Watch for Kreupelenstraat on your left. Turn into it and about half a block on the right enter an arched passage next to the small brick church. The *Chapel for the Blind* is now a Benedictine chapel. Blind citizens lived in adjacent almshouses. Immediately on the left is a small door through which you can enter the chapel. The front door is generally locked.

Suspended from the center of the nave is a ship. According to legend, during the famine of 1502-03 starving citizens had given up all hope of surviving when a large ship carrying grain miraculously appeared and they were saved. In gratitude, a replica of the ship was carved of wood and has hung in the nave of the chapel since that time.

During the 1570's, the Calvinist Beggars of the Sea, based in Ostend, came into the city and destroyed icons and church interiors. A great deal of damage was done to this church, but the lovely marble statue of the virgin and child from the 1300's escaped. The painting below the statue is from the 17th century.

Leave the chapel through the side door and turn left. Behind wrought iron gates on both sides of the walkway are tiny gardens of the *almshouses*. Every community of almshouses has its own garden and a chapel, both maintained by the city. Residents of the city-owned homes for the poor and elderly live free of rent, utilities, and maintenance.

Exiting on Kamerstraat, note an entire row of almshouses, side by side. *Godshuis Voet and Godshuis Van Paemel* were probably named for the donors. *Godshuis Blindekens,* created for the blind by Count Robert of Bethune in 1303, was one of 80 groups of almshouses in use in the Middle Ages. Forty-seven are still used as housing, mainly for the elderly.

Return to Smedenstraat; continue toward the Center City and cross onto the *Zand.* In the Middle Ages, the square was the venue for jousts and tournaments including the lavish celebrations that followed the marriage of Charles the Bold to Margaret of York. Today it is the site of Wednesday and Saturday markets. Hotels and restaurants stretch along the Center City side. On your right, a short distance away, a large modern bronze fountain symbolizing modern Bruges dominates the square. Just beyond, rises the new performing arts center in contemporary architectural design, a source of considerable controversy among the townspeople.

If you reach the Zand at lunchtime, you may want to stop at any of the numerous restaurants facing you. For the budget conscious, the set menu for the day, i.e., the dagmenu or dagschotel, is an excellent choice at many of the restaurants.

Turn left as you leave the restaurant and left again at the first street. Follow it through an arch past modern brick structures. Continue straight through the parking lot until you come to *a lovely garden,* a triangle of lawn and low shrubs watched over by fourteen Stations of the Cross carved into marble pillars. Straight ahead, a crucifix, surrounded by the grieving Marys is flanked on either side by benches, a good place to rest, reflect, meditate, or whatever suits you. Immediately ahead the gothic *dispensary of Saint John's Hospital* is shadowed by the soaring tower of *Our Lady's Church.*

Follow the walkway to Mariastraat and turn left, then immediately right onto the Dijver. You are now in the general area of the original settlement that became Bruges. Watch for narrow Groeninge Lane. Turn right. You will pass the gate to the Gruuthuse garden on the left and the Groeninge garden on the right. Continue as the street winds to the right. Through the wrought iron fence on the left at the canal, you may see swans grooming themselves. At Kastanjehoomstraat and Groeninge seven tiny workers houses in cream with black shutters hug the street. They may, at one time, have been almshouses. Across Groeninge Lane, note the yellow and salmon brick house constructed in 1662.

Continue to Nieuwe Gentweg, perpendicular to Groeninge Lane. Two groups of almshouses, *Godshuis Saint Josef and Godshuis Meulenaere* face you. Godshuis Meulenaere, built in 1613 consists of thirty-one tiny houses surrounding a quiet, formal garden. Low box shrubs, four benches, brick paths and a chapel that faces the courtyard combine to give a wonderful sense of tranquillity.

Exiting the almshouse garden, turn left, continuing on Nieuwe Gentweg one block to its junction with Oude Gentweg and the *Diamond Museum*. Diamond cutting and polishing originated in Bruges. The museum will give you the flavor of the wealth of the city under the Burgundian dukes, a quick history of the town and a lesson in diamond polishing. The first mention of diamonds occurred in 1370. Jewelers of Bruges were among the rich upper class and were involved in both trading diamonds and working with them.

Turn left as you leave the museum and left again on Mariastraat. Proceed a few feet to Wijngardstraat and turn right. It is time to stop at one of the outdoor restaurants on

Wijngardstraat for mussels, Belgian fries, a glass of Straffe Hendrik beer, and a rest for your weary feet. Finish the walk near the beguinage. Find a bench, watch the swans glide along the canal, then close your eyes and drift back to the 15th century.

Glossary

Count - The office of count was roughly equivalent to that of an English earl or an American governor.

County - The area governed by a count.

Duke - The ruler of a duchy. For example, the Dukes of Burgundy were sovereigns of the duchy of Burgundy as well as Counts of Flanders. The title may also designate a military commander as in the Duke of Alva.

Estates General - A representative body made up of delegates from the three great medieval cities: Ghent, Bruges, and Ypres. In the 14th century, the Franc of Bruges was added.

Feudalism - The economic and social system of medieval Europe in which the vassal swears fidelity to the lord who grants the fief and does homage to the lord. The lord owes the vassal protection and respect. The vassal owes the lord counsel and aid, including financial aid and military assistance under certain circumstances. Medieval Netherlands was released from its feudal relationship with France in 1529.

Fief - Feudal estate; something over which one has rights or holds sway.

Franc of Bruges - A territorial subdivision of the county of Flanders with its own administrative, financial and judicial authority. The Franc of Bruges became the Fourth Member of the Estates General after the cities of Ghent, Bruges and Ypres in the 14th century. Today it is known as the Liberty of Bruges, translated from the Flemish *Brugse Vrije* and from the French, *le Franc de Bruges.* The countship of Bruges was divided into several agricultural areas known as *vrijheden,* (liberties), the *Brugse Vrije* being the largest and the most important.

Franks - Germanic tribes from the east and north of the Netherlands.

Hanseatic League - An organization constituted of merchants from free German cities doing business abroad with the object of securing greater safety and privileges in trading abroad. Later, it included the cities as well as the merchants.

Hanse - A trading association

Low Countries - Approximately present day Holland, Belgium and Luxembourg.

Netherlands - Roughly equivalent to present day Holland, Belgium and Luxembourg. Synonymous with Low Countries.

Outport - A harbor or port outside the limits of a main port or customhouse jurisdiction.

Serf - A condition of hereditary and involuntary servitude. In the Middle Ages, many serfs were descendants of slaves or became serfs due to poverty or the need for protection by a lord. Serfdom disappeared from Western Europe in the fourteenth century.

Southern Netherlands - Approximately present day Belgium and Luxembourg.

United Provinces - Present day Netherlands (Holland).

Vassal - A person who renders service, generally military service, in return for a fief.

Bibliography

Belgium: A Country Study. Ed. Stephen B. Wickman. Washington, D.C.: American University. 1984

Bennett, Janet. “Bruges.” Europe. March, 1994

Cali, Francois and Jean-Pierre Sudre. Bruges: The Cradle of Flemish Painting. New York: Rand McNally & Company. 1964

Carson, Patricia. The Fair Face of Flanders. Ghent: E. Story-Scientia. 1969

Dixon, Laurinda. “Van Eyck.” International Dictionary of Art and Artists. Ed. James Vinson. Chicago: St. James Press. 1990

Gaunt, William. Flemish Cities: Their History and Art. New York: G.P. Putnam’s Son. 1969

Geirnaert, Noel and Ludo Vandamme. Bruges: Two Thousand Years of History. Bruges: Stichting Kunstboek bvba. 1996

Gibson, Hugh. Belgium. New York: Doubleday. 1939

Gilliat-Smith, Ernest. The Story of Bruges. London: J.M. Dent & Company. 1905

Goornaert, Can. R. The Beguinage of Bruges. Ed. De Wijngaard, Bruges. 1999

Jacobs, Roel and Jan Vernieuwe. Bruges: The City Behind the History. Bruges: Marc Van De Wiele Publisher. 1997

Letts, Malcolm. Bruges and Its Past. London: A.G. Berry. 1924

Nicholas, David. Medieval Flanders. London: Longman Group UK Limited. 1992

Prevenier, Walter and Wim Blockmans. Tr. Peter King and Yvette Mead. The Burgundian Netherlands. Cambridge: Cambridge University Press. 1986

Rodenbach, Georges. Bruges La Morte: A Novel. Tr. Philip Mosely. Paisley, Scotland: Wilfion Books. 1986

The Beguinage: de Wijngaard Monastic Community. Bruges. Regensburg: Verlag Schnell & Steiner. 1998

The Encyclopedia of the Middle Ages. Norman F. Cantor, General Editor. New York: Viking. 1999

Van Biervliet, Lori. "2000 Jaar Brugge, de Bruggelingen en Hun Vreemdelingen. Waar Is De Tijd. Volume 5: 1998

Wagret, Paul. Polderlands. Tr. Margaret Sparks. London: Methune LTD. 1959

Weale, W.H. James. Hubert and John van Eyck: Their Life and Works. New York: John Lane Company.1908

Webster's New International Dictionary, Second Edition Unabridged. William Nielsen, ed. Springfield: G and C Merriam Company. 1952

Index

Notes

* * * * * * * * * * * * * * *

Beautiful Bruges

* * * * * * * * * * * * * * *

Quick Order Form

Telephone orders: Call 530 756 1475 Have your credit card ready
Email orders: m.attwood@sprynet.com

Postal orders: Adrian Publishing
4447 Cowell Blvd. #11
Davis, California

Please send ____________ copies of Beautiful Bruges: A Traveler's History.

Price/copy:

	USD	Euro
1-2	12.95	14.00
3-5	10.35	11.20
6-9	9.00	9.80
10+	7.75	8.40

____

Shipping by air: $4.00 for first book, $2.00 for each additional book. International: $9.00 for first book, $5.00 for each additional book ____________

Sales Tax: Please add 7.25% for books shipped to California addresses ____________

Total Due: ____________

Payment: Check or money order made out to Adrian Publishing

Credit Card: Visa or Mastercard

Card Number:____________________________ Exp. Date ____/____

Name on Card:____

Address:____

City:____________________State:__________Zip:______ Country_____

Telephone:____

email address:____